CIRCUS PRESS AGENT

Roland Butler, America's foremost circus press agent, promoted scores of acts and attractions for nearly 40 years, including the Wallendas, Zacchinis, Ubangis and Gargantua the Great.

CIRCUS PRESS AGENT:

The Life and Times of Roland Butler

by

Gene Plowden

The CAXTON PRINTERS, Ltd.
Caldwell, Idaho 83605
1984

Library of Congress Cataloging in Publication Data

Plowden, Gene.
    Circus press agent.

    1. Butler, Roland, 1887–1961. 2. Press agents —
United States — Biography. 3. Circus — United States —
Biography. I. Title.
PN1590.P7P55 1983   659.2′97913′0924 [B]   83-21023
ISBN 0-87004-299-8 (pbk.)

Lithographed and Bound in the United States of America by
The Caxton Printers, Ltd.
Caldwell, Idaho 83605
140999

Also Author of

Those Amazing Ringlings and Their Circus

Merle Evans, Maestro of the Circus

Gargantua, Circus Star of the Century

Singing Wheels and Circus Wagons

CONTENTS

INTRODUCTION

IF MY WIFE and I had not cleaned out our garage this book might never have been written, for on that pleasant Sunday we found we had a treasury of material on Roland Butler, America's foremost circus press agent. He lived and worked in a time of circus giants and stood tall among them.

Butler and I had a close personal relationship for twenty-seven years, saw each other frequently, and corresponded regularly. In the scores of letters he wrote, he often enclosed clippings, photographs, and other circus matter he deemed of interest.

Why I saved all this I still don't know, but I seldom throw away anything in the way of printed matter. So there it was — in a steel filing cabinet and a footlocker from my Navy days of World War II, in large envelopes and cardboard boxes.

In completing the book I had valuable assistance from many sources, most of them authorities on the circus and its people.

Foremost was the late Gene Christian, who joined the circus in 1918, later worked on newspapers in Miami, and went back to the circus in the 1930s. He was a close friend and neighbor of Butler, who called Christian "that cheese and crackers agent who never got out of the tall grass and tank towns."

Also Joseph T. Bradbury of Atlanta, Ga.; Gordon M. Carver of Madison, N.J.; Arthur M. Concello, Freddie Daw, Merle and Nena Evans, C. Herb Garrido, John Hurdle, William W. Perry, L. Wilson Poarch, Jr., Elwood Talley, and J. R. Whyte, all of Sarasota, Fla.

Also Jim Garrity of Palmetto, Fla.; F. Beverly Kelley of St. Louis, Mo.; the late Floyd King of Macon, Ga.; Robert W. McCall of Phoenix, Ariz.; Henry Ringling North, now living in Switzerland; Tom Parkinson of Savoy, Ill.; Fred D. Pfening, Jr., of Columbus, Ohio; Charles D. Seip of Allentown, Pa., and Arthur C. Spellman of West Palm Beach, Fla.

My sincere thanks and appreciation to all of them.

GENE PLOWDEN

Sarasota, Fla.

CIRCUS PRESS AGENT

CHAPTER ONE

"HOW TH' HELL can you publicize 'The Greatest Show on Earth'?" Roland Butler rasped in a moment of frustration, looking up from his drawing board where a new likeness of Gargantua the Great was taking shape. "It's like tryin' to blow up a sunrise, by God!"

The crusty press agent for the Ringling Bros and Barnum & Bailey Circus was putting final touches on pictures and text glorifying the latest star of the tented world. It was mid-March, and Butler obviously was irritated.

Normally by this time he'd have checked into the Piccadilly Hotel in New York to trumpet the show's opening in Madison Square Garden around the first of April, but administrative decisions had delayed his departure from winter quarters in Sarasota, Florida.

We had dropped in at the musty old press office (converted years earlier from the Pullman car Alf T. Ringling traveled in until his death in 1919) to say good-bye to a good friend and wish him another season of blue skies and straw houses.

Two of Butler's co-workers had gone on ahead, and others would join them after a winter of promoting plays and motion pictures. When the season got under way there'd be six or seven in his press department, including his good wife, Estelle.

Butler stepped to the nearest window, raised the glass, and looked out upon the 186 acres of winter quarters, where officials, performers, and workingmen were busy getting ready for another eight months on the road.

Nearby, several elephants, under the urging of Hugo Schmitt and his assistants, were shuttling railroad cars into and out of the long paint sheds. Soon these would be assembled into 4 trains of approximately 25 cars each to haul the show to 125 cities in 30 states and Canada before returning to winter quarters in late November.

Butler described them as "double-length steel railroad cars especially built to accommodate the largest circus in the world." In the early 1930s the Interstate Commerce Commission ordered that steel replace wood in railroad cars for safety reasons.

On this March morning the sprawling winter quarters seemed to be a compound of confusion and feverish activity. At the elephant kraals, trainers put the swaying pachyderms through their drills, while in the nearby outdoor training ring known as "Little Madison Square Garden" liberty horses were being taught new and intricate routines.

Scattered about was the rigging, where pretty girls in shorts and blouses swung and swayed in cadence; trapeze artists worked on wires and swings hung between palm and pine trees; ballet girls danced and sang in an airy old building near the paint house.

In the cavernous main building — this once was the Sarasota County Fairgrounds — cage and parade wagons were jammed on one side of the ground floor, while on the other were cages and pens holding tigers, lions, panthers, pumas, seals, and the ponderous hippopotamus.

On the second floor were thousands of costumes glittering with beads and spangles, cut and sewn to fit every human figure in the cast. In the sail loft above, workers had spent months converting canvas into some fifteen acres of new, flame-proof tents, including the gigantic Big Top, which covered three rings, the hippodrome track, and seats for ten thousand spectators.

Two young women worked packs of dogs out near the enclosure where polar bears wallowed among blocks of ice. Giraffes stalked about their fifteen-foot-high enclosures a few yards away.

Boys and girls curried and petted Shetland ponies in the shadow of the main building; hungry and thirsty workers swarmed around the grease joint (lunch wagon). Herds of horses, zebras, and camels grazed in pastures out back.

On a grassy plot at the end of the parking lot Capt. William Heyer put his magnificent black stallion, Starless Nite, through training routines, as he'd done all winter — until the horse would respond to a single word or gentle flick of a whip to dance, kneel, and bow to the audience from both sides of the center ring.

The calliope, parked near the entrance to the main building, had been blaring all morning with "Walking Mike" Doyle at the controls. He'd earned the nickname by walking the three miles from downtown Sarasota every day to play what circus folk called "the steam organ" and put everyone within hearing distance in the mood for a banner season.

The whole atmosphere was county fair, and it would prevail 'til the end of the year.

George W. Smith, general manager; Pat Valdo, director; Fred Bradna, ringmaster; Merle Evans, bandmaster, and others would put this whole mishmash into a fast-moving production lasting exactly two

hours and twenty minutes from opening spec to grand finale.

The entire company of some 1,200 people of 30 or more nationalities from around the world, plus hundreds of wild and domesticated animals, was so well organized and self-contained that it could roll into town at daybreak, erect its acres of tents, stage a two-mile-long street parade, give afternoon and evening performances, and be gone by midnight — duplicating this week after week in cities across the land.

It was not like the movies, a carnival, or a medicine show; this was the circus, a vast gathering of rugged men and determined women, out to entertain and make a living at it. Such was Roland Butler's love and workplace — Ringling Bros and Barnum & Bailey Combined Circus.

Some say the circus was born in the Colosseum in Rome nearly two thousand years ago, but it may have originated long before that, when children in the commune or caves whimpered for entertainment.

Family circuses toured Europe for generations before they reached America. French literature records that a man named Loyal, a street entertainer before joining Napoleon's army, acquired some surplus canvas after the war and set up the first circus tent in France. The Loyals still perform incredible riding feats.

One of the first circuses to reach America was that of John Bill Ricketts, featuring acrobatics and bareback riding. President George Washington is reported to have seen it in Philadelphia in April 1793.

Such entertainment soon spread to New York, Hartford, and Boston, Baltimore and Washington, then south to Richmond, Charleston, and Savannah. As America grew, circuses expanded and multiplied.

They traveled over muddy and dusty roads by night and cruised up and down the Ohio, Mississippi, Missouri, and Tennessee rivers to visit Cincinnati, Louisville, St. Louis, Memphis, and New Orleans.

Circus ballyhoo artists — Frank Braden *(left)* and Roland Butler, top circus publicists, shown in the old press car at winter quarters in Sarasota in 1943. The press car was originally Alf T. Ringling's private Pullman.

Finally they reached Mobile, Pensacola, Apalachicola, Dothan, Tallahassee, Thomasville, and Augusta, bringing the citizenry a variety of entertainment they had never known, including dramatic presentations, comedy acts, trained animals, and good music.

These were not dubious and temporary operators but experienced actors and musicians. They often were greeted with enthusiasm and played return engagements.

Outstanding among them was Dan Rice, a performer so talented and popular that he was proposed, but failed to win, as a candidate for the Republican presidential nomination in 1868.

Phineas T. Barnum, who operated a museum in New York City and toured the country with General Tom Thumb, a midget, and Jenny Lind, the Swedish Nightingale, had a traveling show later called "Barnum's Asiatic Caravan, Museum and Menagerie" prior to his circus venture.

Other circuses of that time included Spalding & Rogers, the first to travel by rail in 1856; John Robinson, Seth B. Howes, Isaac Van Amburgh, Levi J. North, and others. Barnum did not put his "Museum, Menagerie and Hippodrome" on rails until 1872.

Several railroad shows gave him competition, among them Adam Forepaugh, John Robinson, and the Sells brothers. Another was the Cooper & Bailey Circus of James E. Cooper and James A. Bailey.

Cooper retired in 1881, and Bailey, who was to become one of the most capable circus operators of his time, joined Barnum and his brother-in-law, James L. Hutchinson, to launch Barnum & Bailey.

Meanwhile, five Ringling brothers out of Baraboo, Wisconsin, went on tour in 1882 as Ringling Bros. Classic and Comic Concert Co., billed as "A refined and high class entertainment of the most prominent features of the musical and comedy world." Four others were in the cast, and they played small towns in Wisconsin, Iowa, Minnesota, Nebraska, and Illinois.

At the end of the 1884 tour in April, they joined Fayette Lodavick Robinson, better known as Yankee Robinson, to go into the circus field. Yankee Robinson had trouped for fifty years, had owned and lost two circuses, but now was short of cash although still widely known and highly respected in the circus business. It was a ten-strike for the Ringlings.

The first performance of "Yankee Robinson and Ringling Bros. Great Double Shows, Circus and Caravan" was given in Baraboo on Monday, May 19. The Ringling brothers were Albrecht or Al, Alfred Theodore or Alf T., Otto, Karl Edward or Charles, and Johann or John.

Yankee Robinson gave the show prestige and experience, but he didn't last out the season. The old trouper became ill and died in Jefferson, Iowa, on September 4, 1884.

The brothers from Baraboo started the next season's tour in their hometown as "Ringling Bros. Great Double Shows, Circus, Caravan and Trained Animal Exposition," owned by John, Charles, Alf T., Otto and Al. Notice that the names were reversed from the first season.

They were trying to match the flamboyant Barnum and the industrious, hardworking Bailey, and they boasted that they offered "a most gigantic and tremendous aggregation of acrobatic equestrians performing feats of breathless wonder."

Small cards bearing the Ringling name were presented to traveling men, then known as "drummers," which would admit the bearer to any performance. Thus, the drummer would spread the word that the Ringling Circus was coming, arrange his route to meet it, and perhaps bring guests. This created goodwill and helped business.

The Ringlings refused to play on Sundays and acquired the nickname, "The Sunday School boys." They liked it, and the public approved, claiming some traveling amusement enterprises needed to be cleaned up.

John Ringling, two months past his nineteenth birthday, went out ahead on July 25, 1885, to scout for the best stands and pave the way for the show to appear. He usually represented it as "A little bitty thing put on by my kid brothers," thus getting concessions such as licenses reduced or canceled, and use of lots for nothing.

Some who agreed to let the "boys" use their property were furious when they saw the size of the circus, but by this time John was in the next county.

In the spring of 1888 the Ringlings bought the title to the Van Amburgh Circus from Hyatt Frost, who was broke at the time. They went out as "Ringling Bros. and Van Amburgh's United Monster Circus, Museum, Menagerie, Roman Hippodrome and Universal World's Exposition."

They dropped the Van Amburgh title at the end of that season, after playing only Wisconsin and Illinois, but they made 141 stands and took in more money than ever before.

In 1890 they came out with a railroad show of two advance cars and sixteen more for the circus, billed as "Ringling Bros. United Monster Railroad Shows, Great Triple Circus, Museum, Menagerie, Roman Hippodrome and Universal World's Exposition." They traveled by rail on their first invasion of the East, to Ohio, Pennsylvania, Maryland, and Virginia.

That fall they bought more land for winter quarters, added some railroad cars, canvas, and stock, hired a brass band, and boasted they had 130 horses and ponies, plus eighteen cages of wild animals, as well as elephants, camels, zebras, bovalapus, and a yak. They also hired their first full-time press agent, Willard Coxey.

The 1891 tour began at Baraboo, as usual, and the show's title was "Ringling Bros. World's Greatest Railroad Shows, Real Roman Hippodrome, Three Ring Circus

and Elevated Stages; Millionaire Menagerie, Museum and Aquarium; Spectacular Tournament, Production of Caesar's Triumphal Entry into Rome."

On April 7 that year P. T. Barnum died at age eighty-one, but Bailey and Hutchinson carried on as they had for several years, competing not only with the Ringlings but with Buffalo Bill, Sells Bros., Adam Forepaugh, and others.

Bailey was recognized as a brilliant organizer and financier, and by 1895 he owned both the Barnum & Bailey show, with Barnum's heirs, and the Adam Forepaugh Circus.

When the Sells Bros. Circus returned from Australia in June 1892, Bailey let them have the Adam Forepaugh title for one-third interest, and it went out as "Adam Forepaugh and Sells Bros. Great Combined Shows." It competed with the Ringling show at forty-five stands.

John Ringling liked the populous East and proposed they establish winter quarters in Philadelphia as Forepaugh-Sells did in Columbus, Ohio. The brothers would have none of it and expanded winter quarters in Baraboo.

They rented the John Robinson Circus, a well-known and established show, and sent it out with John Robinson, Jr., and Henry Ringling as co-managers. John Robinson's widow said years later, "The Ringlings stole it."

At the end of the 1897 season James A. Bailey took the Barnum & Bailey Circus to Europe, leaving Buffalo Bill, Forepaugh-Sells, and others to fight the Ringlings and John Robinson. When he returned in 1902 he found that the Ringlings had grown to 500 people and that the circus traveled aboard more than 60 cars.

The five brothers, proud and strong, operated collectively like fingers on a hand, forming a powerful fist when necessary. They were in the prime of life, Al at fifty years of age and John, the youngest, at thirty-six.

Bailey, approaching sixty, was still the master circus operator, and he realized no good would come from fighting the Ringlings. Peter Sells died in 1904, leaving only Lewis of the four brothers. Peter's estate had to be settled, and Lewis was anxious to retire.

The Ringlings wanted to buy the Sells brothers share of Forepaugh-Sells, but Bailey balked. He announced it would be sold piece by piece at public auction at winter quarters on January 10, 1905, and issued a catalog listing every single item involved.

Prospective buyers assembled in Columbus on the appointed day, but nothing happened. Bailey bid $150,000 for the lot, and nobody raised it.

Later Bailey sold the Sells brothers' share to the Ringlings, making them partners in the profitable Forepaugh-Sells operation.

When "Ringling Bros. World's Greatest Shows" opened in the Coliseum in Chicago on April 5, 1906, John Ringling hurried east to look over the situation in New York, Philadelphia, and nearby stands.

John was friendly with Adam Forepaugh, Jr., a Philadelphia native who had been featured earlier in his father's circus as "The world's foremost elephant trainer, who can no more have a peer than two suns can exist."

The Ringlings were anxious to buy Bailey's share of Forepaugh-Sells, and luck was on their side. Within the week, James A. Bailey died and was buried.

CHAPTER TWO

THE RINGLINGS didn't waste any time. They made a deal with Bailey's widow and became sole owners of the Forepaugh-Sells Circus on July 1, 1906. Forepaugh-Sells was a first-rate show, and with their own circus they could give Barnum & Bailey tough competition.

George O. Starr managed the combined show in 1906, but it was a disastrous tour with continuous rain early and a blowdown at Iowa City, Iowa, that left it in ruins. W. W. Cole managed it the next year, but a depression was on and business wasn't much better.

The Ringlings were the only experienced showmen with enough money to buy Barnum & Bailey, the great old outdoor amusement enterprise. In October 1907 they paid $410,000 cash for "The Greatest Show on Earth."

They now owned the three leading circuses in the country, and if performers wanted to work and be certain of a payday they had to sign with one of the "big three."

Al Ringling went to Bridgeport to look over Barnum & Bailey's property, and he ordered his agent, Al Freeman, to sign everyone who wanted to work at a flat 10 percent cut in pay.

The Ringling Bros. "World's Greatest Shows" opened the season in New York's Madison Square Garden, while the Barnum & Bailey "Greatest Show on Earth" went from Bridgeport to open in Chicago, each aboard eighty-four cars.

By this time more than thirty circuses were touring America by rail, ranging from about two cars to fifty. If a smaller show beat the Ringlings to a stand, they'd let loose a blizzard of advertising urging the public to "Wait, wait for the Big one — After the minnow comes the whale."

Competition was so fierce that in December 1910 officials of a dozen circuses met in White City, a Chicago suburb, to discuss ways to curb it and to eliminate unsavory dealings with the public. They posted $50,000 bonds to guarantee performance, but, before the next season had passed, the agreement had been forgotten.

They were sometimes called "The Ruthless Ringlings." The designation was due to their rigid rules of conduct and employment contracts, which no doubt came from John M. Kelley, a boyhood friend they hired as attorney to fight a flock of lawsuits.

Kelley said he found more sympathy in federal courts than in local or state, and he won 99 out of 100 cases he defended. For some thirty years or more Kelley was known as "the fixer."

He drew up an employment contract as strict as a military order. The fifty-one rules of conduct the Ringlings adopted covered all employees' behavior, not only on the lot but in all public places.

Females were ordered to dress properly, conduct themselves like ladies, register in their sleeping car before 11 o'clock, and never leave after registering. They must not stop at hotels or visit with relatives and friends without special permission of the ballet master.

Males and females must not talk or visit with each other except with management; the excuse of accidental meetings, even on Sundays in parks, theaters, and restaurants, would not be accepted.

Merle Evans, circus band leader for fifty years, recalls that when he wanted to marry a ballet girl he asked permission from Charles Ringling, who had hired him. Ringling gave his consent.

The employment contract bound the employee to the season's end; it noted risk in travel and services to be performed, and it freed the circus and railroads of any and all claims, demands, and damages, even for gross negligence.

The clincher was a single paragraph of 317 words of legalistic prose stating employees would be furnished transportation and board of the kind customary in the circus business and thus would "receive special personal benefits from such employment."

It added that neither the railroad nor circus management would be liable for any claims for injuries, accidents, sickness, or damages of whatever nature sustained in such service.

The Ringlings made bundles of money with their three circuses. When they went home to Baraboo each fall, it is said, the brothers gathered around the family dining table and passed out profits like dealing cards in a poker game.

Once, during a run on the Bank of Baraboo, the bank president sent a telegram to Charles Ringling, who showed up with a suitcase full of cash. The bank stayed in business.

First of the seven brothers to pass on was August or Gus in 1907 at age fifty-three. Never an active partner, he was in charge of an advertising car.

First of the circus quintet to go was Otto, financial genius of the clan, who nursed every dime they took in. Otto once suggested they buy land in every city they visited, as an investment and to have a place to show, but the brothers turned him down. His share of the circus went to brothers Al and Henry. The latter had been in charge of the Forepaugh-Sells Circus for some time.

Otto died in March 1911, and the Forepaugh-Sells Circus went off the road at the end of that season. The brothers concentrated on Ringling Bros. and Barnum & Bailey, operated them separately, lived in style and comfort, and money poured in.

Albrecht or Al Ringling, who had led the brothers into the entertainment field, occupied one of the largest and finest homes in Baraboo and also built a theater there before his death on January 1, 1916.

John Ringling, out ahead surveying business conditions in all parts of the country and cultivating friendships with promoters and politicians, had astounding good luck wherever he went.

He went into partnership in an oil exploration deal during a poker game one night in Austin, Texas, and a gusher came in. In Ardmore, Oklahoma, he bought land out toward Lawton to mine grahamite, but before the railroad could reach the mine, oil was discovered on his land, and the town of Ringling was born.

John paid a visit to this friend, Ralph Caples, in Sarasota, Florida. He liked what he saw and invested heavily there, buying islands in the bay, stretches of beach property, a fine hotel downtown, and sixty-six thousand acres of land along the Myakka River.

Alf T. was interested in a development in the Florida Panhandle between Crestview and Milton called Floridale. He planned to raise wild animals there for the circus menagerie, but he passed away in 1919 and the project never materialized.

Henry maintained a winter home at Eustis, in central Florida, but died unexpectedly in 1918.

Meanwhile, after World War I broke out

Charles Ringling, one of the five founding brothers, who hired Butler after he worked for Sparks. The latter claimed Ringling "stole Roland Butler from me."

in Europe in 1914, the supply of European performers dwindled, as nearly every country on the continent became involved.

When the United States declared war on Germany in April 1917, the Ringlings commenced to feel wartime shortages and transportation problems.

The two big circuses continued on tour, promoting Liberty Bond drives, entertaining servicemen and women, and sending hundreds of able-bodied young men from their shows into service.

In 1918, while World War I was still raging in Europe, an influenza epidemic swept the United States, killing thousands of all ages and sending millions to bed. The Ringlings realized it was time to consolidate.

For years they'd protested high taxes in Baraboo and threatened to move winter quarters. Combining the two circuses would give them a reasonable excuse.

The Ringling Bros. World's Greatest Show ended the 1918 tour at Waycross, Georgia, on October 8. The Barnum & Bailey Greatest Show on Earth closed the same day in Houston, Texas.

Both headed for Bridgeport, Connecticut, where they were blended into Ringling Bros and Barnum & Bailey Circus, with some 1,400 in personnel, herds of horses and other animals, along with their cages, wagons, and trucks. All were to move on 100 railroad cars in four trains.

When Alf T. Ringling died on the last day of October that year, a substantial portion of the Ringling Circus empire passed from the founders to their wives and children, but Charles and John ran the show.

Charles was in command on the lot — a friendly, understanding man who liked violin music and being addressed as "Mr. Charlie." He did not wish to be called "Mr. Ringling," because to him and many others that meant John.

Charles never quite escaped the shadow of his younger and more flamboyant brother. If he made a decision John opposed, he'd refer to the latter as "my big brother."

The circus was his life, and he was usually with the show from the start. He kept his promises and often complimented an executive or performer for a job well done. He was "with it" all the way.

When the circuses were combined, he hired Merle Evans as band leader — a job that lasted through 1969. The *International Musician* estimated that Evans played to 165,120,000 persons during that time, stating:

"He has probably played to a larger number of actually present persons than any other single entertainer in history."

Charles had many admirers and friends on the show, while others liked John's boldness and daring, his imagination and flamboyance. Charles was on the lot aboard his Pullman, the Caledonia, facing all the problems of operating the largest circus in the world.

John was out ahead aboard his Pullman, the Jomar; at ringside for a championship fight or at a plush hotel, meeting leaders of the business, entertainment, or sporting world; working on business deals that usually ended to his advantage. To the general public he was "Mr. Ringling," symbol of the circus.

Into this complex and capricious world of outdoor entertainment, led by two brothers of divergent attitudes, came Roland Butler, generally regarded as the foremost circus press agent of this century.

His lively and fruitful imagination, talent with brush and pen, wizardry with words and phrases, plus his enthusiasm for the job, propelled him to the top in the glory days of those wonderful traveling organizations.

For forty years he scattered superlatives across the land, luring patrons to tented arenas for an afternoon or evening of clean, wholesome entertainment for the entire family, to be relished and remembered a lifetime.

John Ringling about the time he hired Butler again in 1929 after his brother Charles had passed away. Ringling was circus king at the time, having bought out his major opposition.

Some compared Butler to Barnum, but there were few similarities. Both New England born, they entered the circus field rather late in life — Barnum after touring with General Tom Thumb, the midget, and Jenny Lind, the Swedish Nightingale, and Butler after working on various newspapers and later as a press agent in Boston.

Barnum had his first autobiography printed in London in 1855 and added chapters in later years. Butler never authored a book and discouraged anyone who suggested writing about him.

"Hell, there's nothing newsworthy about me," he'd grumble if a reporter wanted to do a story on him. "I'm just a damn press agent tryin' to do a job. Anything about me would have to be phony if it had any appeal to your readers, and I'd rather not have it. Maybe later."

Often called an advance man or bill writer, Butler was both, but he preferred the more comprehensive title of press agent, promoting everything about the circus he was paid to represent.

As a newspaperman and son of a newspaperman he became known and welcome in every city room in America. Editors and columnists relished his blurbs and ballyhoo because he came in like a surge of fresh air and left them laughing.

City editors, reporters, and photographers were his friends, but he could not abide anyone who called himself a journalist. The very word sent his blood pressure soaring.

"A damn journalist always reminds me of some sissy wearin' spats and carryin' a cane," he'd growl. "I like newspaper men and women to be down to earth; regular folks, by God!"

He could be blunt as a fist in the face, blustery and positive with a flair for the sensational. His responsibility as a press agent was to emphasize the positive and appealing, present a pleasing image, and never acknowledge the negative — to always look ahead to sunny days.

Circus people were rugged and tough; still are. They maintain close family ties, and from birth teach their children obedience, discipline, and hard work. Their pride and independence come from generations before them.

Roland Butler admired these qualities; he belonged.

CHAPTER THREE

ROLAND CHILD BUTLER — he never used the middle name and seldom the initial — was born in Wayland, Massachusetts, a few miles west of Boston, on June 2, 1887, by which time the Ringling Bros. Circus was well into its fourth season.

Roland's father, Harry W. Butler, was working on a Boston newspaper, and his mother was a Wayland native, Loretta M. Eaton. The family soon moved to New Bedford, where Harry Butler became managing editor of the *New Bedford Standard,* the town's leading newspaper.

Roland attended public school but admitted he never liked the classroom. As he grew older he spent more and more time around the newspaper office, running errands, working as a copy boy, and drawing sketches to be used in feature columns and advertisements.

"I learned a hell of a lot more there than I ever did in school," he said.

At the age of fourteen he enrolled in the Swain Free School of Drawing and divided his time between classes and the newspaper office, filling in when the *Standard's* cartoonist was off.

One day he attended a baseball game and watched the Lynn team whitewash the New Bedford Whalers by a score of 9 to 0. Back at the office he stopped in the men's room, and there on a windowsill was a can of cleaning compound called Soapine. The trademark was a black whale with a splash of white on its side.

He drew a whale to represent the New Bedford nine and showed the Lynn players busily whitewashing it. The sports editor liked it.

"The cartoon idea I got from that can of Soapine started it all, I suppose," Roland groused in recollection. "It was a grease and ink remover that printers used for cleaning up after work — a damned useful product, by God!"

New Bedford did not offer the opportunities or appeal of a big city, and when he was eighteen Roland returned to what he affectionately called "Bean Town," where he got a job on the *Boston Globe.* He was there on April 18, 1906, when a great earthquake devastated the city of San Francisco.

Reading reports of the catastrophe as they came in by telegraph, he went to the library and studied pictures and descriptive matter until he was familiar with the city's skyline.

He sketched prominent buildings with smoke and flame spurting from doors and windows, people fleeing in panic, and firemen dragging water hoses through the rubble. The *Globe* spread the drawing across page one, and readers congratulated the paper for the graphic display.

During the following years Roland worked on all the Boston papers at one time or another — *Globe, Post, American,* and *Herald-Traveler* — in art, editorial, or advertising departments.

"I made all of 'em; some more than once," he recalled. "I did a lot of travel and entertainment stuff as well as art work, for Christ's sake! I wrote reviews of movies and plays; a lot of crap about the Berkshires and the Cape — anything to fill in around the ads and dress up the sheet, you understand?

"When I got tired of one paper I'd move on; maybe for better hours or a little more money. It wasn't hard to find work in those days if you could draw and write worth a damn."

A tattooed ship on his right forearm was not the result of a voyage to some foreign port or even a tattoo parlor.

"Hell, no!" he thundered when asked about its origin. "I got the damn thing one night at the *Post*. Another fellow and I were foolin' around in the art department, and I like a damn fool let him put this thing on with India ink. Wish to hell I'd never done it."

Butler and a friend left Boston in 1911 and went to St. Louis, where both expected to find work in newspaper offices. It didn't pan out for Roland, but he met a pretty, blonde, seventeen-year-old switchboard operator at the Marquette Hotel. Her name was Estelle King, and they fell in love.

Roland returned to Boston, but he couldn't forget Estelle. He went to work as amusements editor on the *Herald-Traveler*, saved a little money, and went back to St. Louis, where he and Estelle were married. They rode into Boston as a happy honeymooning couple.

Butler's mother had attempted to break up the romance; now she disowned him. Later Loretta Butler came into a sizable inheritance, including a choice piece of property in Morristown, New Jersey.

"I never got a dime," Roland confided to intimates. "I was cut off completely."

He went to work for Klaw & Erlanger, one of the country's largest and most powerful theatrical syndicates. The company not only booked shows and important entertainers into theaters but also handled advertising for a percentage of the gross re-

turns. Klaw & Erlanger controlled several theaters across the country and even made a few motion pictures.

Through the years 1919 and 1920 Butler turned out program covers, advertisements, and other matter for Klaw & Erlanger from an office at 1020 Metropolitan Theater Building in Boston.

One of his customers was a "shooting gallery" operator from Haverhill, forty miles up the coast, who dealt in motion pictures. The shooting gallery was so called because movies in those days required a long throw to put images on a screen. A long, narrow, vacant storeroom was ideal and usually could be rented at a reasonable cost.

"This fellow came back several times," Roland recalled, "and I found out he specialized in dirty movies. The bastard was rakin' in money from the lintheads working in Haverhill cotton mills.

"He tried to talk me into going to Hollywood with him; claimed he was goin' out there to make movies and I ought to get in on the ground floor. I turned him down cold; he didn't even have a clean collar, by God!

"That's where I dropped my candy, I suppose. You know what happened? The old faht went Hollywood, got the right connections, and wound up head of one of the biggest movie-makin' outfits in the country."

Even then the language of the entertainment world was creeping into Butler's vocabulary. One of his productions for Klaw & Erlanger described Harvey's Greater Minstrels as "the most pleasing, satisfying, and surprising of all minstrels. The biggest and best colored show ever organized."

His promotional matter concluded with these words:

"Presenting a charming Octoroon Chorus and an Olio of highest class vaudeville, superior to that offered by any minstrel, white or black."

Roland Butler's first real contact with the circus occurred in 1920 when Tony Ballenger, general agent for the Sparks Circus, asked him to design some program covers for this small but popular show with a long and interesting history.

Charles Sparks was born to an English music hall couple on April 11, 1876, and brought to this country as a child. His mother died when he was seven years old, and he was adopted by John H. Sparks, who had changed his name from Wiseman to Sparks for show purposes.

Some claim Wiseman took the boy's name for his circus, and it made a clever story, but Gordon M. Carver, a circus historian who researched and wrote extensively about Sparks and his circus, denied it was true.

Carver reported that Charles Sparks began working with Sparks Circus when still a child, and when John H. Sparks died in 1903 he became manager of the show.

By 1919 it had grown into a railroad circus. it traveled aboard fifteen cars that season, expanding to twenty-one cars when Roland Butler joined it early in 1921.

Jack Phillips, bandmaster on the show for many years, compiled neat little route books with photographs of John H. Sparks, founder, and Charles Sparks, manager. Several of these are in possession of Merle Evans, Ringling Bros and Barnum & Bailey Circus bandmaster for fifty years.

Many claim that Sparks permitted no grift of any kind, and his show was regarded as one of the cleanest on the road — an assertion many circuses often made.

Sparks had winter quarters at Macon, Georgia, and usually opened and closed the season there. It had eight or nine elephants and a dozen or more cages of wild animals. The show toured Georgia, Florida, and up the Eastern Seaboard to New York, into

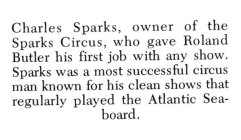

Charles Sparks, owner of the Sparks Circus, who gave Roland Butler his first job with any show. Sparks was a most successful circus man known for his clean shows that regularly played the Atlantic Seaboard.

One of the first and finest letterheads Roland Butler designed for the Sparks Circus in 1921. Note the address where Butler was doing show publicity, and his initials on the design.

Canada, and west to Chicago before heading south, a trip that covered approximately fifteen thousand miles.

Butler's friendship for Ballenger and Charles Sparks was sealed by a letterhead he designed for the Sparks Circus in 1920. It featured faces of a clown and a tiger, with scrollwork in sparkling gold and the words, "A Supreme Achievement in Clean Amusement."

Butler was meticulous in his work and quite proud of this job. One is inclined to think he had a hand in originating the process, or at least was among the first to use it on letterheads. Years later he explained how it was achieved:

Good bond paper was first run through the press with yellow ink, then sprinkled with real gold dust while the ink was still wet. The gold and ink blended, and they still sparkled some sixty years later. Figures

and lettering stand out boldly, and in the lower left-hand corner are the initials, "R.B."

During the following forty years Butler designed and executed scores of letterheads for circuses and other organizations, but none more eye-catching and beautiful than this.

"I left newspaper work because I was sick and tired of bein' an artist," he often grumbled in recollection. "And when I joined Sparks I ran into more goddamn art work than ever. It's a fact!

"Sparks was a successful circus operator — one of the best — and a good man to work for, but I had a lot to learn."

Tony Ballenger was general press agent, Eddie Jackson handled publicity with the show, and Jack Phillips, the band leader, compiled the route book. Butler, the "First of May," did advertising and art work, cal-

Clowns of the Sparks Circus as drawn by Roland Butler, who included himself in the sketch *(upper left)*. His clown faces are still popular as they have been for more than 50 years.

led on newspapers on occasion, and gathered any remaining bits of public relations.

"I was a sort of utility man that first year or two," Butler said, "but you bet your boots there was plenty to do, by God!"

Butler was big and blunt, square-rigged and oak solid. He could act gentlemanly and refined when occasion demanded, or swap stories and salty language with work-ingmen (roustabouts) in a voice that carried like chimes of a calliope.

He wore high-button shoes, gabardine suits, white or lavender shirts, flower-print silk neckties, and broad-brimmed Stetson hats. He could be as soft as goose feathers or tough as buckskin.

He had an open, friendly face, square jaws and a positive chin, blue eyes that sparkled beneath heavy brows, thinning hair slicked down and parted on the side.

Courier cover designed by Roland Butler for the Sparks Circus in 1922, one of the first pieces of art work he did for Sparks.

His mouth was frequently framed in the embryo of a smile, and his laughter was a treat to hear and share.

Many towns the Sparks Circus visited had only weekly newspapers, so the show often came and went before reviews could get into print. Butler realized this and provided the most favorable reviews to editors ahead of the show, aware that some preferred printed copy to writing their own.

Butler and every other press agent worth his pay collected posters, programs, and lithographs to use in promoting the circus

he represented, finding nothing wrong in lifting a picture, a phrase, or even a few paragraphs.

Floyd King, owner, operator, and press agent active in the business for some seventy years prior to his death at age eighty-eight in 1976, described an incident involving Butler, Sparks, and the Ringling show.

"I was in Warsaw, North Carolina, late in the fall of 1922 when I visited Charlie Sparks, who had a fifteen-car show that year and was a good friend of mine," King wrote.

"I spent most of the day with him, and my contracting agent, Ed Shaw, showed up on the lot about 5 o'clock. Roland Butler, Shaw, and myself left on the late afternoon train for Rocky Mount, and Roland continued on to Boston where he lived.

"Roland had a stack of lithographs, and he told Sparks he'd left the press material in the ticket wagon. Roland also had several photographs of the Ringling-Barnum show.

"The following spring Charlie Sparks visited the Big Show in The [Madison Square] Garden, where John Ringling jumped him about using Ringling lithographs. John told Sparks 'I will see you tomorrow.'

"Sparks said, 'Why wait 'til tomorrow? We can straighten it out now.' Sparks told Ringling he would have the lithos destroyed and there would be no further complaint, which I am sure he did."

Butler soon learned of John Ringling's gripe, and from that day on conducted a campaign against the Big Show that did not end until the Ringlings hired him.

CHAPTER FOUR

ADVERTISEMENTS HERALDING the Sparks Circus in the 1923 season shouted, "Ring out the Old; Ring in the New."

"Last summer the residents of Kokomo were surprised and delighted with the Al G. Barnes Circus, which came here as a stranger and made many staunch friends because it presented something NEW," the ads read.

"At that time Kokomo unanimously agreed that old-time circuses and moss-covered circus ideas were a thing of the past.

"On next Monday, August 13th, another circus NEW to this city will make its initial bow to Kokomo — THE SPARKS CIRCUS."

Butler was emphasizing the new against the recently combined Ringling Bros and Barnum & Bailey Circus, as well as others such as John Robinson, Sells-Floto, and Forepaugh-Sells. The Ringling-Barnum show had played Kokomo in 1921 and regularly visited such stands as Terre Haute, South Bend, and Indianapolis.

The Sparks advertisement continued:

"With a thousand and one features NEW to circus audiences, the big Sparks show is coming here. Surprise after surprise and novelty upon novelty will predominate in its performances.

"NEW blood, NEW ideas, NEW equipment, NEW faces and NEW inventions will everywhere be evidenced. It's the last word in up-to-the-minute circus achievement.

"The SPARKS CIRCUS is not 100 years old. It does not operate as circuses did in 1823, and furthermore it does not want to. It has no century old cob-webbed attractions or circus paraphernalia that should have long since been relegated to the dust bins of antiquity.

"It's a circus of 20th Century PEP, just 100 years ahead of any other circus coming within hailing distance of Kokomo this season — and above all it's NEW.

"Note: The enlargement alone of the Sparks Circus this season represents greater financial outlay than the total cost of any 100-year-old circus that ever rattled and squeaked on the North American continent."

Pure Butler prose, it sniped at the older and much larger Ringling show, emphasizing the new against the old. A Sparks courier that season read:

"The 20th Century wonder show. Sparks Circus. This season augmented by the world's finest display of trained wild beasts. Almost half a century of unsullied reputation. A mighty achievement in clean amusement."

Another Sparks advertisement shouted:

"The Canvas Covered Classic, one hundred per cent clean and wholesome; an army of accomplished arenic artists; comprehensive menagerie of perfect zoological specimens; two herds of performing elephants; hundreds of the most beautiful horses ever exhibited."

Butler now had the title of general press

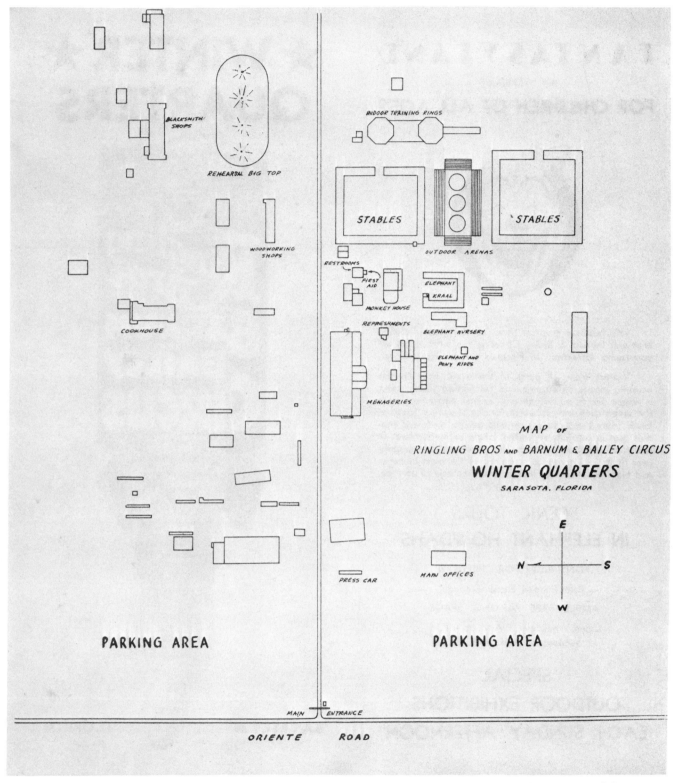

Map of circus winter quarters at Sarasota which Ringling Bros and Barnum & Bailey occupied from 1929 until 1959, when it moved to nearby Venice.

representative, while Ballenger was general agent. L. B. Greenhaw was press agent ahead of the show and Eddie Jackson agent with the show. Harry Mack held the title of advertising press agent.

The Ringlings were mindful of Butler's NEW approach and made efforts to counteract it. An advertisement in the *Billboard,* the show business bible, for April 19, 1924 stated:

"Time tests all things and Ringling Bros and Barnum & Bailey has stood that test for 90 years."

It added that Ringling Brothers had forty years behind it and Barnum & Bailey fifty years, boasting that the two combined had entertained 800 million people "severally and jointly during those years." It called this "a conservative estimate of the grand total of their combined and world-wide audiences."

One of the most popular and attractive features of circuses from earliest times to the 1930s was the street parade — a living, moving stream of beauty and pageantry, flowing to the rhythm of great brass bands — the most powerful and persuasive advertising medium circuses ever had.

The parade usually started shortly before noon, when most people were on the streets. Every detail was carefully planned, and it moved with military precision down the town's main street past the courthouse or town hall, stretching for a mile or more.

The call to parade sounded twenty minutes before the procession was to move off the lot. Everyone was involved in one way or another, each on his or her best behavior.

Riders carrying banners moved ahead, followed by the owner or manager in shiny surrey or carriage, followed by trumpeters and buglers.

There were cages of wild animals; ladies in glittering costumes astride horses of similar size and color; band and tableau wagons; floats, clowns, and men riding high-stepping steeds or driving teams of draft horses.

There might even be a Wild West section with cowboys and Indians; a mounted band; assorted animals, birds, and reptiles; elephants; and finally the calliope, belching smoke and steam.

Circus press agents extolled the virtues of this musical monster, operated by steam or compressed air, and claimed it could be heard ten miles away yet its tones were "softly sweet as a lover's lute."

"Twenty blocks of gorgeous street parade; a vision of beauty and splendor," was Butler's description of a Sparks Circus street parade. They were considered outstanding for a circus of its size, and they continued for years after most circuses discontinued them because of traffic congestion.

Sparks also staged an elaborate opening spec — a parade around the hippodrome track — featuring music by Jack Phillips and his eighteen-piece band, with songs and dancing.

One of Roland Butler's classic promotions appeared that year. It began when he stumbled onto an exciting tennis match at an exclusive club on Long Island, New York. He saw a bevy of young girls lying on their stomachs and sides, peering under the canvas wall outside the stands, skirts tight across their hips and thighs.

Summoning a photographer, Butler had him record the scene. When the photographs were delivered, he sketched in circus props and captioned the results as follows:

"Society notables in unconventional poses see performance of Sparks Circus."

Consulting the Social Register, the press agent selected names at random and scrambled them to identify each young lady as an Aldrich, Astor, Chittenden, Chisholm, Harrison, Morgan, Schuyler, Stuyvesant, Whitney, Widener, or Winthrop.

The picture appeared in newspapers

throughout the country, and the Sparks Circus used it for years.

"It was a beaut!" Butler smiled, and added one of his favorite expressions, "Jim to Mollie."

Although he never met either of them, Jim and Mollie were two of his favorite people, mentioned often in his conversation. He used the expression as a standard of excellence, referring to James A. Bailey and Mollie Bailey, unrelated but both outstanding circus managers.

James A. Bailey was for many years the managerial brains behind the Barnum & Bailey Circus. He worked on a small circus as a boy and in 1874, at age twenty-six became general manager of the Hemmings, Cooper and Whitby Shows. Whitby was killed that same year, and when Bailey bought Hemmings's share the operation became Cooper & Bailey.

P. T. Barnum went into partnership with Bailey in 1880 in a show called Barnum and London. The following season their circus made its debut in New York City as

One of Roland Butler's major promotions in the early 1930s was the Ubangis, a name he found as a river in central Africa. Chief Neard is at extreme right, and three musicians in front.

"Barnum & Bailey, The Greatest Show on Earth."

It is one of the most imaginative and effective slogans ever conceived and now has been used for more than a hundred years.

While Jim Bailey was considered the most capable circus man of his time, Mollie Bailey was his counterpart among women. When Gus Bailey, operator of a little mud show, died in 1896, his widow, Mollie, became manager as well as owner.

She not only raised several children, some of whom became accomplished musicians, but converted the show into a railroad circus in 1908 and operated it successfully until her death in 1918.

In Butler's estimation, Jim and Mollie were supremes of the circus world.

Charles Ringling supervised overall operation of the giant Ringling Bros and Barnum & Bailey Combined Circus from his Pullman, the Caledonia, from the start of the 1919 season until his death.

He was familiar with Roland Butler's work and added him to the press staff commencing with the 1924 season. Butler was to work under the veteran general press representative, Ed Norwood.

"My big brother probably won't like it," Charles warned Butler, "but I know your work and we can use you."

John Ringling roamed the nation in his Pullman, the Jomar, when he and his wife, Mable, weren't in Europe booking circus acts and buying art. He could travel free on any line in the country because he had invested in railroads and at one time owned four small lines — in addition to oil wells, ranch lands, and beach property.

Money from these, plus the circuses, enabled him to acquire some six hundred old masters which cost, by his estimation, more than $11 million.

The Ringlings still owned the Forepaugh-Sells Circus. When John met it in Tampa, Florida, late in 1911, he continued fifty miles down the coast to visit his friend, Ralph C. Caples, general agent for the New York Central Railroad, in the town of Sarasota.

John bought a home on Sarasota Bay and convinced Charles it was the smart thing to do. Charles agreed, and the brothers helped the sleepy fishing village of 1,200 grow and become a popular wintering place for people of wealth, including the Palmers of Chicago, the Karl Bickels of New York, the Bill Selbys of Denver, and others.

Through the years the Ringlings bought considerable property along Sarasota bay and its beaches, sixty-six thousand acres along the Myakka River, and an island in the bay called Bird Key.

There was only one large house on the key, and John had that prepared as a winter White House for his friend, President Warren G. Harding, who agreed to vacation there early in 1924 but visited Alaska in the summer of 1923 and died in San Francisco en route back to Washington.

John and Mable built a fine place on Sarasota Bay patterned after the Doges Palace in Italy and called it Ca d' Zan or "House of John." In 1947 it became a state museum, along with the John and Mable Ringling Museum of Art, which had opened in 1931, the same time the Ringling School of Art and Junior College was founded.

Charles built and moved into a plush house near John's mansion, which later became the nucleus of New College.

John became president of a bank, and Charles opened one of his own; John had a yacht, the *Zalophus II*, and Charles cruised aboard his yacht, the *Symphonic*. John was involved in spectacular projects on Lido, St. Armand's, and Longboat keys.

Charles bought a golf course on the edge of town, and it became a subdivision. He donated land for the county courthouse and built a hotel a block away, to rival one John had bought on the other side of town.

Charles Ringling fell ill at his Sarasota home and passed away on December 3,

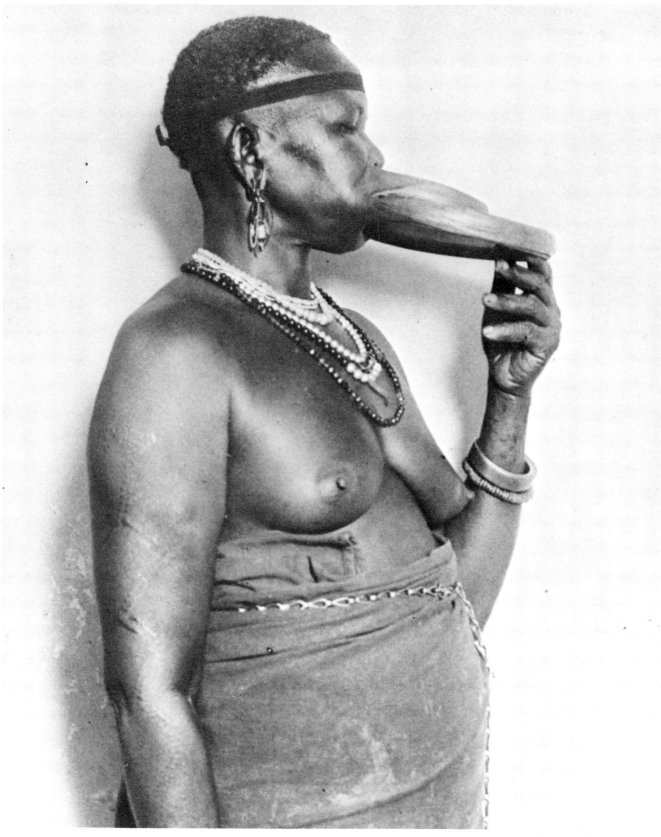

Princess Aimidon, one of the saucer-lipped Ubangi women featured on the Ringling Bros and Barnum & Bailey Circus in the early 1930s, was one of Butler's favorites.

1926. John was at his bedside and mourned that "I'm the only one left."

John Ringling had groused about the lithograph episode of 1922, as Charles predicted. Now he remembered it and other publicity jabs Roland Butler had taken at the Big Show while working for Sparks. With Charles gone, the press agent was promptly dropped from the Ringling payroll.

CHAPTER FIVE

CHARLES SPARKS enlarged his circus a bit for the 1927 season and was happy to have Butler back in the press department, working with Harry Mack and Bruce Chesterman.

The show traveled aboard 20 railroad cars with 400 in personnel, including 27 men in the advance car. Walter McClain, who later was on the Ringling show, was the elephant handler and a good one. Producing clown was Paul Wenzel, with more than a dozen funsters in his crew.

Butler's hand was evident in newspaper stories, ads, and other printed matter hailing the Sparks outfit as "America's tented masterpiece; Bigger and Better than ever this season." It was billed as "The Greatest Amusement Achievement of the Age, now augmented by the world's finest display of wild beasts."

Note Butler used the word "beasts," a more positive term than "animals." He carefully chose language for the best effect.

In Detroit that season he pulled off one of his classic promotions. He met Forrest D. Freeland, staff artist on the *Detroit Free Press,* and they hit it off splendidly. They photo-duplicated a picture of about sixty horses at the unloading runs, practically doubling the Sparks equine strength and earning an eight-column spread in the newspaper.

This display of horsepower generated strong interest in the motor capital of the world and caused John Ringling to sputter because his circus was due in Detroit a few days later.

Deeply involved in Sarasota promotions, he decided to move circus winter quarters there. John had proposed this earlier, but Charles objected. Now that Charles was gone, John shared ownership with the widow, Mrs. Edith Ringling, and Mrs. Aubrey Black Ringling, widow of Aft T.'s son, Richard. It was "Mr. Ringling" who ran the show.

John Ringling had such an infatuation for the town and county of Sarasota that he pushed vigorously for concessions to bring the circus in. His friends, Ralph Caples, A. B. Edwards, and A. E. Cummer, held a $50,000 mortgage on the old fairgrounds and agreed to forget it if the circus moved there.

When the Ringling Bros and Barnum & Bailey Circus ended its 1927 tour in Tampa on November 3, the four-train caravan rolled through town and three miles east to the facility it was to occupy for the next thirty-two winters.

Sam Gumpertz, a close friend of John Ringling, managed Eugene Sandow, the strong man, and Harry Houdini, the escape artist. He was a rough rider with the Buffalo Bill Show and the builder of Coney Island's Dreamland and Brooklyn's Brighton Beach.

Gumpertz told Ringling of a sensational act then in Cuba, and the pair went to Havana, where Ringling signed the Karl Wallenda troupe. It then included Karl and

While the circus had winter quarters three miles from town, executive offices were upstairs, over John's Bank of Sarasota, in a wedge-shaped building at Five Points in the heart of town.

Butler occupied a tiny office down the hall, a few steps from the pie-shaped cubicle Ringling maintained at the pointed end. Butler did much of his work in his modest home in Midway Grove, a spread of orange and grapefruit trees a short drive from winter quarters.

He saw the busy, opportunistic "Mr. John" infrequently. The circus king slept until near noon, then ate a large and leisurely breakfast before attending to business. His activities included drilling for oil about twenty miles south of Sarasota, building the Ritz-Carlton Hotel on the south end of Longboat Key, and completing his sprawling art museum and palatial residence.

John Ringling loved animals, especially if they were large and had box office appeal. He often walked about the grounds of his mansion with a pet monkey or parrot perched on his shoulder.

About 1916 the circus exhibited a gorilla named John Daniel, for which it reportedly paid $10,000. It had another named John Daniel II in 1924. Neither lived very long, for little was known about the feeding and care of these great apes at that time.

The first real animal attraction Butler was called upon to promote was an elephant seal, or what the press agent called "a gigantic sea elephant." It was a carniverous animal with a trunklike proboscis, found in the Pacific Ocean off North and South America.

This specimen reportedly cost Ringling $30,000 and was first exhibited in 1928.

"Build him up; make him bigger than all hell," Ringling told his press agent. "He's

Pfening Collection

After the Ubangis returned to their native Africa, the circus featured these so-called giraffe-neck women from Burma, discovered by circus scout Howard Y. Bary.

Closeup of one of the giraffe-neck beauties from Burma, showing the copper rings worn around the neck with dangling earrings.

got to live up to the name Goliath, you understand?"

Butler turned out posters and window cards in vivid color and a rotogravure folder on Goliath. He ordered bales of printed matter for the season. Picture captions read:

"GOLIATH, the mammoth sea elephant, the only one of its kind ever captured and exhibited alive. Now one-third larger than last season and growing at the rate of a ton a year!"

Reporters, zoologists, and others ap-

peared at winter quarters asking for details and pleading for a look at the great sea elephant. Roland was ready with a logical explanation. He said Goliath was off the coast and it would take some time and effort to bring him ashore, which would not be done until the show was ready to leave.

The press agent had rapport with an Associated Press writer in New York, who inquired by telegraph if it were true that Goliath was ailing as rumored. Butler neither confirmed nor denied it but replied: "Sea elephant here eating 400 pounds of fish every meal."

He didn't say how often Goliath was fed. The truth was Ringling put Goliath in an enclosure on St. Armand's Key that allowed the sea elephant to wallow in brackish water or lie on the sand, hoping this would attract buyers to a subdivision he was promoting there.

The real estate boom fizzled, the tropical paradise where Goliath dwelt was deserted, and the bulky mammal passed the winter in virtual seclusion.

When Goliath was moved to winter quarters he was smaller than anyone anticipated and seemed to have been on a starvation diet.

"Holy God!" Ringling cried. "He's a sorry-looking critter; stinks to high heaven, too. What do you think happened to him, Roland?"

"Looks to me like he lost weight instead of puttin' it on, don't you think, Mr. Ringling?"

"Christ, yes; must have lost a ton or more. We can't exhibit anything like this. He's sick!"

Goliath's body was wasting away, covered with white splotches and flesh falling off in chunks. Butler suggested he might have been attacked by an octopus or some other enemy, causing infection, loss of weight, and perhaps more serious ailments.

The sea elephant went to New York with the show that spring, paraded in a large wagon around the hippodrome track a few times, then died. Butler quickly withdrew all reference to Goliath, but when inquisitive reporters asked what happened, Butler was ready.

"Like a damn fool, he stayed in the water too long, by God!" he said. "We believe exposure to fresh air and hot sun then set up toxins. The combination of such massive fat, brackish water, fresh air, and warm sun made the beast toxigenic, experts have told us. Humidity works both ways, you know."

CHAPTER SIX

BUTLER'S PRESS DEPARTMENT had ample attractions other than unusual animals to shout about — May Wirth, Australian beauty and supreme horsewoman; Lillian Leitzel, superb aerialist; Luisita Leers and Winifred Colleano, stars of the flying trapeze; Merle Evans, the colorful and durable band leader from "down home" in Columbus, Kansas; the Wallendas; and many more.

Hugo Zacchini was a sensation as "The Human Cannonball." Wearing aviator's helmet and white leather coveralls, Hugo was shot from the mouth of a monster cannon and arched into a net 90 feet away.

Butler described Hugo as "The human projectile — a living person shot through space with violent velocity from the mouth of a monster cannon. The sensation of the century."

A few years later the act provided new thrills when Hugo and Mario Zacchini used a "monster repeating cannon" to send not one but two human beings zooming through the air.

Such attractions often generated more attention and applause than the riders, flyers, and balancers, who considered themselves real artists, not stunt men and women. It was all part of the circus, but Roland Butler and other press agents were forced to tread a narrow pathway between skilled performers and sensationalism. It's no wonder he preferred to promote animals, especially if they were exotic and oversized.

"Animals can't talk back and hound you for publicity like some goddamn 'artistes,' " he grumbled. "They seem to appreciate the attention and our efforts to promote 'em; not like some temperamental humans always griping and bellyaching about not gettin' enough notice in the press, for Christ's sake!"

Tom Mix, star of Western movies who became a circus performer, was not one of Butler's favorites. John Ringling once testified he paid Mix $10,000 a week for thirty weeks, and perhaps Butler was a bit jealous.

Circus salaries are never revealed, but in its heyday it was rumored the press agent got $12,000 in one season. Officials would only confirm that "press agents never made much money."

When Butler interviewed Mix for press material, he learned the actor was born in Pennsylvania and not in the West as generally believed. Mix first saw that section of the country when he was in high school and visited his grandmother on a Kansas farm, Butler said.

"I had to glorify the s-- of a b----, so I had him born in an adobe hut out on the prairie surrounded by shootin', shoutin' Indians.

"Then I had him holdin' Colonel Lister's head when that old fellow lay dyin' in the Boer War. I even put Mix in the Boxer Rebellion, by God! Had to move him around to give him some color and publicity, you see?

"He'd been a popular movie star but was well past his prime when he came to the show, so I had to build him up into a circus attraction without offendin' his fans. Tom Mix couldn't do a goddamn thing. One time he even fell off his horse and hurt his shoulder. It was taped up for two weeks, by God!"

Mix, then forty-eight years old, did fall and injure his shoulder one night when the show was in Dallas. Reports at the time said his horse slipped on a muddy hippodrome track before taking a hurdle, throwing the rider heavily to the ground.

Mix had such box office appeal that other cowboy movie stars followed him to circuses, among them Hoot Gibson, Tim McCoy, Ken Maynard, and others.

It peeved some other Ringling performers to learn how much Mix was paid — plus having his private car on the Sells-Floto show, then a Ringling property. This luxury usually was restricted to the owner or manager. Even on the Ringling-Barnum show most top executives and star performers considered themselves fortunate to have a stateroom.

Fred Bradna, John Ringling's longtime friend and ringmaster for many years, and his wife, Ella, star equestrienne in the center ring, reported that they lived with sixty-two others in a car on the Barnum & Bailey Circus for eight years before moving into a stateroom.

Jess Willard, world heavyweight boxing champion, had a private car for the short time he was with the Sells-Floto show, but for Willard and Mix to have their own private cars generated jealousy.

The big Ringling Bros and Barnum & Bailey Circus had few private cars and only for the top echelon. Normally it had one stateroom car, where such stars as Lillian Leitzel, May Wirth, Bird Millman, the Fred Bradnas, and others lived. Merle Evans said he was with the show for twenty years before he got a stateroom.

When the Big Show acquired a herd of donkeys, Butler set out to make them a feature attraction. Neither Roland nor Ringling knew where the little animals came from, so the press agent consulted maps and atlases until he found the name "Pongo River" in Africa. He was not sure they came from that continent, but it didn't matter.

"Incredible Pongos!" the billing matter shouted. "Miniature donkeys from the depths of diabolic Africa, bred as war mounts for a blood-curdling tribe of cannibal pygmies!"

They were a popular attraction for a season or two, and that was enough. The circus was always offering new and interesting exhibits, whether human or animal. It was the responsibility of Butler and his staff to promote them to the hilt.

An eastern university heard of the Pongos and wrote for details. Butler replied with a list of measurements approximating those of a greyhound, and described them as gallant little beasts capable of carrying three times their weight through the brush while led by pygmies. It was another of his contributions to the field of animal husbandry.

One of his most successful promotions — prior to Gargantua the Great — was a troupe of big-lipped women from French West Africa who arrived just in time for the Madison Square Garden opening in 1930. The women didn't join at winter quarters but reached New York aboard ship and joined the circus there.

Dr. Ludwig Bergonnier, a Frenchman, was responsible for this exotic importation that included Chief Neard, a stocky, glowering, dark-skinned fellow; his wife, Princess Aimidan; three lesser wives; four other women, and three men.

All the women had grotesque enlargement of the lower lip, achieved by inserting wooden disks in slit lips of girl babies and increasing the size as the child grew. According to Bergonnier, the larger the lip the more beautiful the girl.

Butler was enthusiastic. Here was something he could promote with vigor as one of the most amazing attractions the circus ever had.

"I could get my teeth into this one, by God!" he recalled some years later. "Nothing like it had ever been seen by civilized man; the press had a field day. Believe me, it was a pip!"

He searched a detailed map of Africa and came up with the word "Ubangi," from the name of a river flowing into the Congo. He wasn't certain where the attraction originated, but he liked the word and so did the public. He called the women "The world's most weird living humans — new to the civilized world!"

Butler described the latest circus attraction in these words:

"Monster-mouthed Ubangi savages with mouths and lips large as full-grown crocodiles; from Africa's darkest depths!"

The lips on Butler's posters and broadsides seemed to be the size of turkey platters, but in reality, they were more on the order of bread plates or saucers. Some patrons commented on this, but there were other parts of their bodies to gawk at as well as the lips.

The women were between the ages of sixteen and forty-five, and all were substantially built, especially in the chests and hips. They wore garments like beach towels wrapped around the hips and thighs — nothing else.

When they left the ship in New York, hardy dock workers stared in disbelief. They'd seen all manner of imports over the years but nothing like these well-padded women.

The show was ready to open in Madison Square Garden, but these women had no costumes. John Ringling had signed the attraction sight unseen and didn't want to lose any time exhibiting them. He told Bradna to "Send them in as they are; we've got no time to lose!"

When the eight women, nude to the waist, paraded around the hippodrome track few among the thousands in the crowd dwelt on the enlarged lips, including John Ringling.

"My God, Freddie!" he whined to Bradna. "We can't have this; we'll be ruined. Put clothes on them right away. We've got to cover up those big tits!"

Planning advertising and publicity for the big show in the press car when Sam W. Gumpertz was vice president and general manager. *From right to left:* Sam W. Gumpertz, sitting at the desk in foreground; Roland Butler; Frank Braden, veteran story man; Pat Valdo, director of personnel; Col. Ralph C. Caples, advertising counsellor; Bill Cunningham, noted sports writer of the *Boston Post* and *Collier's Weekly*, a visitor; and Mrs. I. W. Robertson, executive secretary to Mr. Gumpertz.

Jeanne Carson, head of the wardrobe department for many years, escorted them to a store in Manhattan and had them fitted with short skirts, pullover sweaters, and shawls. She also bought shoes — the first they'd ever had.

The Ubangi women soon discarded the shoes and sweaters. "Too hot," Bergonnier explained. They agreed to drape the shawls over their shoulders and chests during the performance.

A stage was set up in the menagerie tent where they were on exhibit, and they earned extra money selling postcard pictures of themselves. The circus paid them $1,500 a week, it claimed, and they brought it much, much more.

The Ubangis had no luggage, but Chief Neard had a heavy wooden box with double locks that he wouldn't let out of his sight. It was believed the chief put what money Dr. Bergonnier gave him in the chest and saved it.

Three of the Ubangi men were musicians, or performed as such. Two played bongo drums, and a third had a xylophone hung around his neck. It was equipped with calabash resonators.

"I never did find out where they got those resonators from," Merle Evans reported, "but they sure made a lot of noise."

The Ubangis were housed in one large room with ample beds, flush toilets, and shower baths. They preferred sleeping on the floor, so the beds were moved out. They were terrified of flush toilets and refused to use them. Buckets were substituted. They loved shower baths and used them daily.

The Ubangis proved to be one of the greatest attractions the circus ever had. They toured for two seasons and reportedly returned to their homeland and invested in cattle ranches.

Roland Butler considered the Ubangis one of his best promotions, and he laughed heartily every time he saw the words "Ubangi much?" that naughty boys had scrawled on posters all over the country.

The press agent never missed an opportunity to give John Ringling favorable publicity, although he never liked his boss as a man. Butler had the rare ability to put aside personal feelings when necessary, as if they never existed. In the *Billboard* of May 10, 1930, he wrote:

"This year, for the first time in history, the destinies of America's six foremost circuses are in the hands of one man. Unlike some branches of the amusement business, the 'white tops' are fortunate in being under the direction of a master showman.

"Also, for the first time in recent years, thousands of people in the tented world are entering a season with their minds at ease and with definite knowledge as to just where they stand. This condition was forecast when John Ringling came into control of the circus field last September, and it has materialized."

Roland mentioned such things as individuality, possible expansion, enormous resources, and a healthier circus world, and then launched into one of his favorite subjects — circus paper.

"John Ringling's appreciation of art," he wrote, "will also manifest itself in the printing matter used to advertise circuses of the future. That was inevitable as indicated in a series of new posters heralding 'The Greatest Show on Earth.'

"Last year several styles of circus bills, modernistic in design and of infinitely more artistic value than any previously seen on billboards or in store windows on this side of the Atlantic, were used to advertise the Big Show. The bills were drawn by one of America's foremost poster artists. [He was not identified.]

"To say that these posters created more comment than any circus bills in generations would be a conservative statement. To the public in general they were of an unexpected appearance and consequently did just what they were intended to do —

The "pygmy" elephants were introduced with great fanfare and featured for a year or so before they grew up and became part of the Ringling herd of nearly 50 pachyderms.

attract attention. To those of artistic taste and discernment, they were a delightful innovation. . . .

"It is the ambition of John Ringling to raise the standard of circus posters to a higher degree of artistic excellence than has been attained in this branch of lithographic art."

Butler had a basis for this line of reasoning. Ringling had been quoted as saying he spent $11 million for works of art, was building a museum in Sarasota, and planned to open an art school there.

Butler decried the tradition of circuses advertising themselves with what he described as "bills of riotous, clashing colors and recklessly-thrown-together conglomerations of conflicting detail" and predicted bills of this type were slated to go.

He wrote of "Ringlingizing" executives of his other circuses and claimed the circus

owner was cognizant of the power of the press to produce results, adding:

"Mr. Ringling fully appreciates the unique position the circus enjoys in the entertainment field by being handled as news by the fourth estate."

The Butler essay concluded by stating that "Interesting newspaper stories and illustrations do more to create circus-day enthusiasm than any other form of printed matter."

Butler and his men were always friendly and cooperative with the press and kept it informed of circus activities, especially if favorable. They publicized stars visiting shut-ins, underprivileged children given free admission to the show, and anything else that might benefit the circus.

The *Billboard* of August 6, 1930, reported that John Ringling, just back from Europe, spent a day with the circus in

Chicago and was well pleased with the patronage.

"Excellent publicity has been obtained by the show," the story said. "Three ace press men are on the job — Roland Butler handling the photos, and Tom Killilea and Frank Braden the press.

"They have done a good job of it as attested by the columns of space obtained in the dailies. The Ubangi savages have furnished live copy, and the birth of a baby zebra was a break for the press agents."

Forrest Freeland had caught the eye of Hollywood producers for his promotion of the picture "Trader Horn," and they offered him a job but he turned it down. He had been bitten by the circus bug and called on Roland while the show was playing Madison Square Garden.

Freeland claimed later that Butler agreed to give him a job in the press department provided he would never reveal that he was an artist. Freeland's widow said later her husband returned to their hotel room terribly disappointed and upset.

Butler never commented on the incident, but friends agree it may have been professional jealousy. He was an artist, too, and experienced in the circus field. Big as it was, Ringling Bros and Barnum & Bailey Circus had no need for two artists in those depression years. As general press representative, Butler could lay ground rules.

Later Freeland handled national advertising for Clyde Beatty-Cole Bros. Circus and used letterheads Butler had designed, but the two never patched up their friendship.

CHAPTER SEVEN

The Ringling group now included four circuses traveling aboard 235 railroad cars — Ringling Bros and Barnum & Bailey wintering at Sarasota, and Hagenbeck-Wallace, John Robinson, and Sells-Floto at Peru, Indiana. Jess Adkins, veteran circus owner and manager, was manager of the Peru quarters and later the Hagenbeck-Wallace show.

Butler and his men kept abreast of Sarasota and Peru operations, which included transfer of horses and equipment between the towns nearly 900 miles apart.

Butler and Braden, especially, who worked together in Sarasota quarters, produced a tremendous volume of text and pictures for newspapers, magazines, heralds, programs, posters, and route sheets emphasizing attractions and life on the road.

Butler's clown faces were considered masterpieces and are still sought by collectors. His letterheads were eye-catching — "to grab attention," he said.

In addition to his other duties he carried on voluminous correspondence with people in all parts of the country, often writing four or five pages in longhand to answer a request for information or to exchange news of the moment.

Once when asked how many people he knew personally, Roland thought for a moment, then replied:

"I don't have the slightest idea. I send out 2,800 Christmas cards every year, mostly to newspaper friends, and I know the names of every one of 'em, plus a hell of a lot more."

Circus trains involved interesting facts, and Butler made good use of these, turning out stories on loading, moving, and setting up the city that traveled by night.

The circus owned its cars, but the engines belonged to the railroads over which it moved. Circus trains were treated as "extras," and railroad crews worked closely with circus officials, giving them priority and close attention.

"Why not?" Butler asked. "It's live cargo and brings them a lot of cash. It takes skilled crews to move four trains on our tight schedule, and a hell of a lot of cooperation."

In those days the Big Show used 35 to 40 different railroads to reach 125 cities in 35 states and Canada in a season lasting 220 days and nights. One move was only 10 miles between St. Paul and Minneapolis, but it was 721 miles from North Kansas City to Denver and 718 from Portland, Oregon, to San Francisco.

During those long jumps animals as well as humans must have food and water.

Butler was always alert for any local incident that might bring the circus favorable publicity, as happened in San Angelo, Texas, during the 1930 tour.

A few days before the circus was to arrive, and school to open, a youngster named Scott climbed a tree and threatened to stay there rather than attend classes. Butler heard about it when he called at the newspaper office, and he volunteered to help. The city editor happily accepted his offer.

"We'll bring him down, by God!" Butler swore as he accompanied a photographer, reporter, and some townspeople to the scene. While they surrounded the tree, Roland looked up and bellowed:

"Can you hear me, lad? Can you hear me?"

Nearly everyone in San Agelo could, and did. Butler begged the boy to come down and go to the circus as guest of honor. It took only a moment for the boy to scramble to the ground and accept the invitation. The story and pictures brought the circus valuable publicity.

"That was a beaut!" Butler agreed. "It had a real human interest touch."

In 1932 the circus moved executive offices from downtown Sarasota to winter quarters three miles away. Butler and Braden took over the Pullman that had belonged to Alf T. Ringling, converting it into a press office.

Alf T. had planned displays in every detail — costumes, lighting, and music, some of which he wrote. When he died in 1919 the car remained in winter quarters and was moved to Sarasota in 1927.

During the next five years it was home to transients, including a troupe of performers. Roustabouts lived there and finally a collection of drifters.

Butler struggled to rid the place of these undesirable tenants, who regularly picked the locks or climbed through windows to spend the night with bottles of cheap wine and stale bread scrounged from the cook house, leaving trashy evidence of their sojourns.

The problem was solved only after locks had been changed several times and latches put on windows so they could only be opened from the inside. A crew cleaned and disinfected the musty old coach to make it habitable. There was a sink and commode in back, and a plumber put them into workable condition.

"It looked like a pigsty when we moved in, but now I suppose it'll do for a press office," Butler said sourly after he installed his drawing board, two desks, chairs, filing cabinets, wastebaskets, and an old-fashioned hall tree for hats and jackets.

The car was spotted about 50 yards inside the entrance gate and 100 yards from the main building. Between the press car and main building were car sheds, paint shops, storage barns, and other facilities, laced with spur railroad tracks. An old railroad car housed the show's executive offices, and out beyond it to the left was the cook tent and hospital tent.

The Alf Ringling Pullman was ideally located for Roland Butler and Frank Braden. From desk or drawing board they could screen visitors entering or leaving and could see what went on around the car barns and paint sheds.

If the press agent was busy and not in the mood to entertain, he'd lock the door and scurry into the rest room. When a new season was approaching he had little time for towners, as he called most visitors.

But he was always happy to have columnists and reporters such as Robert Lewis Taylor, Courtney Ryley Cooper, Bill Cunningham, Henry McLemore, Earl Chapin May, and Ernest Hemingway. Ned Roberts reported for the *Billboard*.

Arthur Brisbane, one of the leading editors and columnists of the time, often wrote about the circus, and his columns were given prominent display in many newspapers.

Butler once asked Roger Babson, a highly regarded financial writer, to produce a column about the circus. The town of Babson Park in central Florida was named for him.

Babson noted that all circus people were optimistic, never knew despondency or fear, were always cheerful, and never doubted that tomorrow would be better than today or yesterday, and he urged all

Americans to adopt the same attitude and outlook.

The Great Depression was on, and Babson's columns reflected his feelings that there were better times ahead.

While the circus was "at home" from late November to mid-March, Roland worked alone until five or six weeks before the tour began, when Frank Braden joined him. Braden was a veteran storyman and publicist; they were long-time friends and worked well together.

Other members of the press corps might come in for a few days before the show was to leave, to look over winter quarters and review plans for the season, or they might join in New York.

Butler had a rich storehouse of stories from many sources — contracting agents, advertising and traffic personnel, performers, twenty-four-hour men, the circus "fixer," in the donnikers (rest rooms), around the "grease joint," and the virgin car, where sixty-six ballet girls lived on the road.

He collected these with relish, like others look for stamps or autographs, and was always happy to share them. Braden was a neat, quiet man who said little but joined in Butler's laughter.

Roland worked as if surrounded by malefic devils; each task must be finished today. He was never known to relax and could endure silence only so long. Then he'd break out with a laugh, recall out loud a funny incident or story, and conclude his recitation with a deep, chesty guffaw.

If something nettled him, he'd explode in

Author Gene Plowden (left) with Roland Butler outside the old press car at Sarasota winter quarters in 1948.

a burst of profanity that could be heard across the big parking lot and into the main building fifty yards away.

On a typical morning Estelle would drive him to the press car around 7:30 or 8 o'clock, give him a good-bye kiss and exchange a parting word. He would gaze after her as the car pulled away, then turn and rush up the steps, jam the key into the lock, shove open the balky door, and drop his battered old brown briefcase on the floor beside his desk.

Then he'd stride to the rear of the car, hang his suit jacket and Stetson hat on the clothes tree, and fumble in a pocket for his packet of Camel cigarettes, which he smoked in moderation.

While the car was still trembling from his jarring footsteps he would loosen his necktie, unbutton his shirt at the collar, and roll up his sleeves halfway to the elbow.

Roland probably preferred Camel cigarettes for a personal reason. He liked to tell how John Ringling, who bought Havana cigars by the gross and usually nibbled on one, was a friend of R. J. Reynolds up in Winston-Salem, North Carolina, and put the picture of a dromedary on the Camel cigarette package.

According to Butler, when Reynolds planned to manufacture a cigarette blended of Turkish and domestic tobaccos, Ringling presented him a photograph to use in advertising. It was of a dromedary in the circus menagerie; the true camel has two humps, not one.

"Reynolds didn't know any more about camels and dromedaries than Mr. Ringling did," Butler said. "When the cigarette called 'Camel' came out with that picture on the package, both took a lot of ribbing; people even wrote in pointing out the difference.

"Reynolds said, 'What did they know about camels? My friend John Ringling's got practical knowledge, not something out of a book. Anyway, we'll use his camel; one hump's enough.'

"When the dromedary died," Roland concluded, "damned if they didn't have it mounted and put on display in the foyer of the factory. The mangy old thing may be there yet, for Christ's sake!"

The mail would be brought in, and Butler would attack it with his usual vigor, clipping off the ends of envelopes with a large scissors to get at the contents.

"We always try to answer as much of our mail as possible the same day we get it, or the day after," he explained. "Otherwise we'd be swamped with all this crap. Frank [Braden] takes care of a lot of it. He'll be in directly."

Letters came from all parts of the United States and a few from Canada, inquiring about everything from the date the show was to appear in a city to measurements of an elephant's foot; from weight and age of certain midgets to how much and how often a tiger is fed. One writer said he knew all about Barnum but nothing about his partner Bailey. "Please tell me all about him."

Roland put aside several letters and went to work on others, using a fountain pen and writing in a bold hand. A few minutes later he telephoned the main office, in a railroad car nearby.

"Hello!" he shouted into the mouthpiece. "This is Roland Butler over in the press department; who'm I talking to? Oh, yeah. How are you? I just got word Zacchini is gettin' in Monday. You say Otto Griebling got in? Good.

"Is Mr. Valdo there? Ask him to call me when he gets in. All right; I'll be talkin' to you later. Good-bye."

While Butler was on the phone Braden breezed in, nattily dressed as usual — starched white shirt with cuffs showing below the sleeves of his gray double-breasted suit, diamond stickpin in his necktie, glistening gold cuff links, diamond ring on his finger, and Homburg worn at a rakish angle.

A smallish man, Braden was qualified both by education and experience. He'd at-

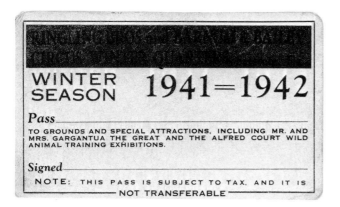

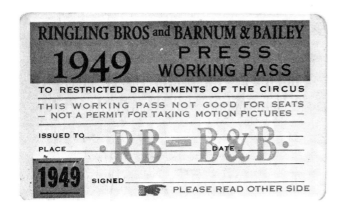

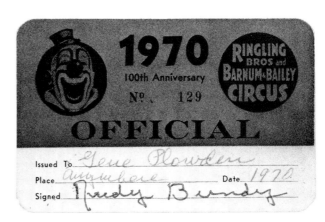

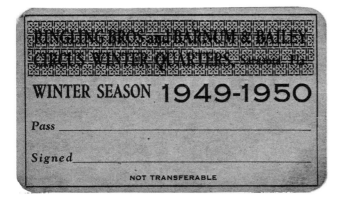

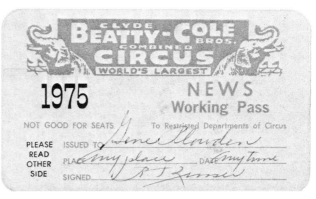

Working press passes issued to writers and photographers allowed them into all parts of the circus, although they were not good for seats. The press was always welcome at the circus.

tended the Naval Academy at Annapolis, Maryland, served as a U.S. Cavalry officer with Joseph W. ("Vinegar Joe") Stilwell in the Philippines, then turned to press agentry for movie and stage productions and circuses.

Braden stood ramrod straight, walked with military precision, and spoke in a soft, soothing voice. Once he placed a midget on the lap of J. Pierpont Morgan, the international banker, while an alert photographer snapped a picture that appeared in newspapers all over the world.

Newsmen claimed that Braden always carried a shoebox full of circus tickets into city rooms along with his stories and left them there. Anyway, he got results.

Butler and Braden worked steadily in the press car until noon, Roland at his drawing board and Braden hammering out releases and answering letters on a battered old Underwood.

"By God, Frank," Roland exclaimed. "We've got to do a piece on that new act, the Zavettos. They tell me it's a thriller. I almost forgot about it, to tell you the truth."

"Good idea," Braden agreed. "I'll get on it soon as I finish off Doc Scully, the vet."

"Hell, yes, give Doc a good sendoff," said Butler. "Everybody knows John Scully. The story'll get front page play in the *Trib*. We'll give it to Ned Roberts for *Billboard*, too."

Butler raised a window and looked out at a pair of elephants shunting baggage cars into and out of the paint sheds. Studying them for a few minutes, he went to work on a sheet of drawing paper 24-by-32 inches, long side up.

Using quick, bold strokes, he outlined the massive rear of the larger of the two swaying only a few steps away, pausing to moisten the tiny brush with his tongue,

dabbing here and there to get the proper shading. The large, graceful curves made him smile, and he drew the tail almost full scale, the size of a baseball bat.

"By God, that's a beaut!" he remarked, standing back to admire the drawing that almost filled the page. "After all, we're featuring a quarter of a million pounds of pachydermous pulchritude, and ought to do it right. Don't you agree, Frank?"

"Right," Braden grinned, glancing up from his work.

"Hey, Hugo!" Butler shouted to Hugo Schmitt, who worked the elephants. "That big one's Modoc, ain't it?"

"Yes, Mr. Butler," the elephant handler assured him. "That's old Modoc."

"Good. Just wanted to make sure we had the biggest and oldest in the bunch. Everybody knows old Modoc, Jim to Mollie.

"Now there's a beautiful behind; a classic, drawn from life, by God. Isn't that the biggest butt you've ever seen? Nothing phony about this one. It ought to go on a billboard instead of bein' squeezed up in a program or route book."

It was lunchtime, and the two press agents walked over to the grease joint for lunch. Butler ordered a slice of pie with ice cream on top and a cup of coffee. Braden popped a couple of pills into his mouth and gulped coffee.

They spent fifteen or twenty minutes at the lunch counter, greeting friends they remembered from other years, watching visitors stroll by, and talking about who'd be returning for the coming season.

"By God!" Butler pounded the counter with his fist. "I've got to get busy on that new attraction Howard Bary's bringin' in from Burma — the savages with the long necks. That should be a pip."

CHAPTER EIGHT

EXPLORER BARY had sent photographs to Butler. Taken in the jungle, they showed the women surrounded by what appeared to be family and friends on an outing. Closeups of five or six women showed them with brass rings around their necks.

The tiny, gentle creatures, reportedly captured in the wilds of Burma, were not ordinary human beings in Butler's estimation — nothing was.

"Royal Burmese Giraffe-Neck women," his billing matter read. "The greatest educational attraction the world has ever known!"

These maidens, Butler wrote, were captured while roaming the Burmese jungle searching for men, and the brass rings kept the men from choking them. The traditional sport of "necking" caused the elongated necks.

Butler took a roll of solder wire, wound it around big wooden spools, then superimposed pictures of the women's heads and faces above the spools, making their necks resemble those of baby giraffes. When seen on gaudy circus posters, they appeared to be two feet long!

Posters, heralds, broadsides, and other circus literature pictured the women in colorful dress, with brass rings not only encircling their necks but from wrists to elbows, and on knees, calves, and ankles.

The Burmese women lasted two seasons, billed as "The last of the unknown peoples of this earth. A thousand years behind our epoch!"

Butler's day ended at 5 o'clock when Estelle picked him up. By this time he was completely exhausted, but after a good night's sleep he'd be ready for another day's work.

One veteran storyman and all-round press agent who reported to winter quarters two weeks before the show left was Dexter Fellows, a medium-sized, rotund man with a bristly gray mustache, noted for his charisma among newspapermen and women.

Fellows had worked for Barnum & Bailey, left it to do theatrical publicity, then returned to the Ringling combine.

A dapper figure in gray fedora or straw skimmer, Fellows usually wore a gray suit, checkered vest with heavy gold watch chain stretched across his middle, and white or pearl gray spats. He carried a gold-headed cane, which he twirled in debonair fashion, breezing into newsrooms like the showman he was.

The story of his visit might go like this:

"Spring arrived in town today. Dexter Fellows blew in from Florida, and that means Ringling Bros and Barnum & Bailey Circus is not far behind. This giant of the outdoor entertainment world, offering many new and exciting features according to Mr. Fellows, is due in two weeks."

This bit of news likely as not would appear beneath a picture of Fellows, complete with hat, cane, and cigar, or there might be a column or more devoted to the dapper press agent and the circus he represented.

When in Sarasota, Fellows visited the *Sarasota Daily Tribune* and his friend, Managing Editor Earl Stumpf. He'd be invited to sit in as telegraph or city editor, and he relished the attention. Fellows kept abreast of the news, was familiar with all kinds of stories and sizes of type, and would even edit copy and write headlines.

He might spend an hour or more, and the afternoon edition would have a story about him and the circus. This doubtless irritated Butler, who was businesslike and brief during his visits. It also was thought to create some friction and even jealousy between them.

Fellows once wrote a circus book in which he apparently intentionally avoided any mention of Roland Butler. When this was called to Butler's attention after Fellows had departed, the crusty old press agent shrugged his broad shoulders and, in the Boston accent he never lost, declared:

"Evidently the old faht never liked me."

In addition to the triumvirate of Butler, Braden, and Fellows, the circus had three or four other experienced press agents each season, some for many years.

Most prominent of these — and the only one still alive as this is written — was F. Beverly Kelley, whose specialty was radio. Kelley was head of the press department for a few years when both Butler and Braden left following a change in management.

Kelley arranged for the first circus records ever cut (Victor), co-wrote and narrated seven consecutive Fitch Bandwagon shows on the NBC radio network featuring Merle Evans and his band.

The versatile press agent also wrote about the circus in the National Geographic Society's magazine and coauthored several circus books.

Circus Hall of Fame Collection

The two Butler children are shown in this rare photograph, Estelle at left and Edward at right.

"I had great admiration for Roland Butler's talent, and I learned from him as I did from Dexter Fellows and Frank Braden," Kelley said recently.

Another member of the press staff, as long as Butler was in charge, was his wife, Estelle, who was Butler's chauffeur and companion. Roland never learned to maneuver an automobile, and while she drove he rested and prepared to invade newspaper offices in the next town. He estimated they averaged about twenty-five thousand miles a season on the road.

Plump and with a pretty face, Estelle was squarely built, exuded enthusiasm and good humor, and was known for her candid comments and repartee. If one wished to see her glow with happiness, all he need do was greet her with, "Estelle, you've lost weight since I last saw you!"

"Do you really mean it?" she would ask, smiling. "Oh, thank God! I hope you're right; you know I have a weight problem. Tell Roland, will you?"

They complemented each other and spent more than forty happy years together. She called him "Roland" and he called her "Estelle" or "Stelle." Frank and friendly, they chose friends carefully and kept only a few. They were circus all the way.

Among others in the press department from time to time during Butler's years were Arthur Cantor, A. J. Clarke, William Fields, Eddie Jackson, Bernie Head, Don McCloud, William H. Roddy, Allen Lester, and Gardner Wilson.

Merle Evans, who led the circus band for 50 years, is shown with his wife, Nena, and life-size portrait by Donald Rust, in collection at Ringling Museum of the Circus.

When Kelley was not available, the radio department was managed by William Antes or Frank Morrissey, aided by Norman Carroll or Charles Schuyler.

Butler usually left winter quarters two weeks ahead of the show, checked into the Piccadilly Hotel in downtown New York, and had his publicity staff in full operation when the circus came in.

On the day the show left winter quarters, Father Charles Elslander of St. Martha's Catholic Church in Sarasota, accompanied by a score of children, appeared on the scene to bless the trains. This little ceremony continued for many years.

When the trains passed through downtown Sarasota on their way north, half the population lined the right-of-way, waving and shouting "Good-bye and good luck. See you in the fall." It meant the end of "the season," and nothing much would happen until the circus came home again.

In those years the whole of Sarasota County had only about 15,000 inhabitants, and the circus was a tremendous financial asset as well as a tourist attraction.

Just before the show left on tour it gave two full, two-hour performances on the grounds of St. Martha's Catholic Church, which reported, "More than 2,000 attended each spring, of which fully two-thirds were non-Catholic."

All the circus headliners participated; admission was fifty cents for adults and twenty-five cents for children, and every penny went to the church.

"Between afternoon and evening performances typical circus snacks and a great supper were served on the 'Midway,' " the story of the church compiled by the parish history committee stated.

"It has been called the church that the circus built."

Many communities across the U.S.A. were circus towns — Baraboo, Wisconsin; Bridgeport, Connecticut; Peru, Indiana; Macon, Georgia; Deland, Florida; Hugo, Oklahoma, and others — but Sarasota led them all.

The Ringlings and their circus were a vital force in the area for more than thirty years until, some citizens claim, "Developers drove them out."

CHAPTER NINE

LONG BEFORE CARS were loaded and the trains blessed, the vast canvas-covered city that moved by night had been planned to the last detail — where and when it would perform, railroads it would use, and provisions it would need. The new tour began when the old ended.

The man most responsible for logistics was the general agent, an individual who knew railroads, lot owners, merchants, and political leaders on the circus route.

He or his contracting agents must know railroad trackage to accommodate the trains, cost of moving them in and out, and location of a suitable lot, preferably close to railroad, street car, and bus lines. The proposed show date must not conflict with fairs, festivals, and other attractions, and the community must not be in a business depression.

City or county permits must be taken out; the show must comply with police and fire department regulations; and provision must be made for water, parking, and other necessities. Agents also contracted with merchants for hay, grain, meat, and other supplies.

All these facts must be reported to the general manager and possibly to "Mr. John" himself, who studied these reports carefully, having once been a general agent himself and knowing the country as well as any man of his time.

Behind contracting agents went outdoor advertising and traffic departments — thirty or more persons aboard three railroad cars.

The billing (billposting and lithographing) department moved in a week ahead to bill all city and country routes.

Aboard the three combination sleeper-workshop cars was at least one contracting press agent who called on newspapers and radio stations, placing advertisements and perhaps leaving a story or two.

Butler's press people used the advance cars for transportation only; they did not work there. The car manager supervised a crew of billposters and lithographers who also distributed heralds, couriers, and, in the old days, "rat sheets" attacking the opposition.

There also was an "opposition brigade" to look for any earlier circus paper that had been covered with opposition bills. The brigade restored these and left men in the city to protect their fresh billing if they felt it necessary.

A crew of "tackers" or "tack spitters" went to the tops of buildings carrying ladders which they let down to tack sheets of printed muslin to the brick walls. They carried a mouthful of tacks which they spit out one by one and whacked with a light tack hammer. Some of these displays could be seen for two miles or more.

Late on circus day a crew would return and, by loosening a corner of a twenty-four sheet, retrieve it. They'd give the sheet a quick jerk and tacks would fly off. The bill would fall to the ground to be folded and used again. These banners were heavily starched muslin colorfully printed on one side. The tacks merely held them to the wall and were not driven in like a nail hammered flush.

Contracting press agents, working under Butler, were concerned only with advertising their circus. Next to them came storymen, usually more experienced and better paid, who worked closer to the show. A "press agent back with the show" got photographers out of bed to shoot unloading and setting up shots for the evening paper.

That agent also met Very Important People and the local press at the front door and escorted them to seats in Section G, the best in the house.

When the circus played Washington, D.C., the president was invited and sometimes accepted — or at least held a little ceremony in the White House to accept the invitation. Among presidents who actually attended performances were Woodrow Wilson, Warren G. Harding, and Franklin D. Roosevelt.

Butler devised a leap-frog system whereby storymen would be ahead two days and back on the show one, giving them a chance to see the show and know what was going on.

Butler also knew that editors responded better when an agent rushed in with a picture and story of a new feature, and then three days later another appeared with a new offering. Editors liked these visitations and often edited and marked the copy for the next day's editions.

Smaller circuses usually had one press agent, and if business turned sour he was the first to go. His duties would be assumed by the contracting agent ahead of him.

Circuses playing towns of fifteen thousand or less had one general or contracting agent who did it all. He either rented a lot and saw the mayor about a license or contracted with a local sponsor.

That sponsor secured a lot and got the license fee waived. If the agent had any

time left in his fifteen-hour day he met officers of the sponsoring group — civic club, police or fire department — and spoke at a luncheon if one was planned. He also called on the town's newspaper, usually a weekly, with a story and cut or mat of the owner or a featured attraction. The agent would pay for advertising with tickets to the performance.

Advance crews withered in the 1930s and by the 1960s had almost disappeared from the American scene. Outdoor billing teams became unpopular with the public. Farmers often refused to have pictures of circus animals plastered on their barns, and storekeepers found other uses for their windows. Cities restricted the posting of bills; some even refused to let circuses come in.

Highway officials claimed billboards created traffic hazards, and some states prohibited outdoor advertising on rights-of-way. Many large "paper houses" or printers went out of business, and the aroma of horse manure vanished in automobile exhaust fumes.

Perhaps it was just as well. A circus agent traveling ahead of his show was not interested in "towners" unless they could help him. "Home" to him was his show, or any other he might visit, where he was welcome and his language understood.

It was a sad thing that association with a circus often alienated one from the life stream of the more settled and accepted gentry and left a man a loner except in a society of his own choosing — a society that in Roland Butler's time was looked upon with suspicion, and often still is.

The general press representative was busy every hour of the day, out front doing his job, and had little time for socializing. Few people, even on the show, had the opportunity to know Roland and Estelle Butler very well.

During the season they usually were miles ahead of the show, and when it was in winter quarters they kept mostly to themselves. They were friendly enough

Roland Butler *(left)* and his wife, Estelle, chatting with Norman bel Geddes *(center)* who designed many of the circus sets.

politicians in ever city the circus visited, but he knew little of day-to-day operations. After he bought the American Circus Corporation the Great Depression set in, and John Ringling went downhill, physically and financially.

His first wife, Mable, died in June 1929. He went off to Europe, where he met and courted a wealthy widow named Emily Haag Buck. When she returned to New York he was there to meet her, and he insisted they get married at once.

The ceremony was performed by Mayor Frank ("Boss") Hague of Jersey City in his office on December 19, 1930, but not before John had borrowed $50,000 from Emily, putting up one of his paintings as collateral. All this happened, Hague said later, on the day of the wedding. Later the painting was sold for $95,000.

John and Emily didn't get along, and he finally won a divorce in July 1936. This cost him, in legal fees, $211,000 — a record for a divorce in Florida up to that time. Emily received one dollar.

John suffered a thrombosis but showed remarkable recovery and managed to keep an eye on the circus, although he had not an ounce of authority on or off the lot.

The year was 1932, and Ringling, grumpy and ill with gout, lost control of his circus empire when he failed to pay on his loans held by Allied Owners, Inc.

Samuel W. Gumpertz, Ringling's old friend, was named executive vice president and general manager. John remained president, but it was in name only, at a salary of $25,000 a year.

What had been a Ringling operation for most of fifty years was now in alien hands; Gumpertz was not a Ringling by blood or marriage. Gumpertz and his wife had stayed in John's house for three years before building their own home in Sarasota; then their friendship curdled.

"Gumpertz was a pain in the ass for the press department from the start," Roland Butler grumbled to reporters. "He had ears like a jackass and was never a top executive like Bailey and the Ringlings."

Unlike the big, brusque, and positive man a circus boss was supposed to be, Gumpertz was a smallish, myopic fellow who parted his hair in the middle, wore thick-lensed glasses, and spoke in a high, squeaky voice.

The press department needed photographs of Gumpertz, and Butler called in a professional lensman from Sarasota who specialized in portraits. When the thin, precise cameraman reported to the press car Roland warned him about Gumpertz's ears and gave him strips of adhesive tape.

"When you're all set up," Butler said, "just step up behind him and slip the tape behind his ears and close 'em up, you understand?"

At the ready, and with no sense of tact or timing, the cameraman ducked from beneath his black cloth hood, walked over to Gumpertz seated in a folding chair beside the office car, and asked in a shrill voice:

"Shall I pin his ears back now, Mr. Butler?"

"Why, Mister———!" Roland shouted, calling the photographer by name. "We brought you out here to take pictures of Mr. Gumpertz, the new executive vice president and general manager of The Greatest Show on Earth, not to insult him and embarrass me. Now, take your goddamn pictures and get the hell out."

CHAPTER TEN

ROLAND BUTLER'S wizardry with words was widely recognized, with such examples as "The Royal Burmese Giraffe-Neck Women," "Sons of the Midnight Sun" from Lapland, and "Unus — the man who walks on his forefinger."

Ardelty performed on a sway pole, and Butler called him "The upside down daredevil in stratospheric flights atop a ten-story buggywhip."

He hailed the Wallenda troupe as "The last word in high wire thrillers. New, hazardous and hair-raising feats by world-acclaimed artists who shake hands with death at dizzy heights."

He publicized everything about the circus, human and animal, from aardvarks to zebras. He gave the world the word "Ubangi" and made Gargantua a star.

In its fortieth anniversary special circus edition of December 29, 1934, the *Billboard* paid Butler this compliment:

"It has often been said that modern circus advertising material lacks the vivid superlatives and stirring adjectives of the 'golden age of circuses,' but is it really true?

"Two generations ago the heralds of the Ringling Bros Circus described the opening spectacle as 'A mighty, moving panoramic display of opulence, grandeur, magnificence and splendor, presented by the new invincible monarch of the circus world — Ringling Bros Stupendous New Consolidation.'

"Quite forceful and lavish, 'tis true, but it

must be remembered that Roland Butler, general press representative of the Ringling-Barnum Combine, is no slouch when it comes to putting together circus publicity copy. Compare the elaborate claims of the 1894 edition of the Big Show with Butler's modest description of the past season's spectacle in those attractive heralds scattered over the length and breadth of the land.

" 'Ringling Bros and Barnum & Bailey Combined Circus, this year reaching the zenith of its glorious reign over all amusements, introducing 1,000 amazing new international features and innovations, including the most sublime spectacle of all time, the Durbar of Delhi, by far the most stupendous and dazzingly beautiful production ever conceived for the delectation of circus audiences.'

"The program called the 'All new 1934 edition of the Durbar of Delhi' the most magnificent spectacular pageant that mankind has ever gazed upon, and did not neglect to mention 'The terrific new sensation presented by the Great Hugo — two living persons actually fired from the mouth of a monster repeating cannon.' "

For the record, the Durbar of Delhi was truly a spectacular exhibit. Designed to duplicate a state reception given by an Indian prince for a British governor in India, the circus version was as lavish and spectacular as money and imagination could make it.

First presented by Barnum & Bailey in 1905, it was revived for the golden anniversary of Ringling Bros and Barnum & Bailey Combined Circus in 1933 — the Ringlings fiftieth year — and presented again in the 1934, 1935, and 1936 seasons.

This display of oriental splendor included the entire elephant herd, plus all performers, animal and human, parading around the hippodrome in gorgeous costumes of every color and hue.

Leading the parade was Modoc, the great old elephant that weighed 9,280 pounds and stood seven feet ten inches tall. Modoc was covered with a blanket of glittering gold and shouldered a howdah in which rode a gilded damsel called "The Golden Girl," surrounded by uniformed and turbaned attendants carrying pennants and spears.

The tournament or "spec" usually opened the performance, set the stage for the productions that followed, and put the audience in a mood to relax and enjoy the show.

Clever billing year after year brought tremendous followings for such performers as Lillian Leitzel, May Wirth, Ella Bradna, Vera Bruce, Dorothy Herbert, Bobby Steele, La Norma, Dolly Copeland, and others. Clowns like Emmett Kelly, Otto Griebling, Paul Jung, Lou Jacobs, and scores more spiced the performance with laughter.

Thrills and spills were assured by the Cristianis, Hannefords, Alfredo Codono, Con and Winnie Colleano, Loyal-Repenskys, Captain William Heyer, and others.

The Flying Concellos was one of Butler's favorite acts. Triple somersaults by Arthur and Antoinette Concello, man and wife, on the same bill was a spine-tingling sight. Considered one of the most difficult of all flying maneuvers, it was achieved only through years of strenuous practice, split-second timing, and great concentration.

Clyde Beatty once had forty lions and tigers in the same ring, and this was billed as "The greatest and most daring wild animal act ever presented."

Alfred Court became famous for his control of ferocious jungle beasts — not by whip, chair, or gun but through kindness and patience. He worked with lions, tigers, panthers, leopards, wolves, and other animals. The same was true of Trevor Bale, who trained everything from bears and tigers to birds and mice.

Butler publicized these and many more, showering them with superlatives season after season, but he remained ever alert for anything to keep the circus in the news.

Before the 1935 season he announced that hereafter all the circus's printed matter would be copyrighted. He knew all circus material had been "appropriated," but his copyright announcement brought some nationwide attention, which probably was his idea all along.

"All new pictures, pictorial matter, and other material will," he announced, "for the first time bear the copyright label, indicating it will be protected by law. A complete file of all new material has been made and sent to the copyright office in Washington.

"And when we say copyright, we mean exactly that. The circus has invested thousands of dollars in new material and, by God, we don't intend to take chances with those pirates who might steal it and with a few alterations use it in opposition to us. It's been done for years."

Coming from Butler or any other circus press agent, this caused some raised eyebrows.

Every real trouper dreamed of some day working for the Big Show. Once on the payroll, some considered themselves "artistes" and hounded the press department. This irritated Butler and Braden, but especially Butler, who was their target.

What galled him and set off volleys of shouting and cursing by the loudest voice in winter quarters was to retouch the face and figure of an aerialist or rider and get not a word of thanks. Likely as not the subject would criticize the result or walk away in silence.

"That's not good of me at all; I want another picture," the offended performer might complain. "I don't think it does me justice."

"Justice, hell!" Butler would bellow. "If you'd slim down that big behind and take some fat off those piano legs it would help. I've done you a favor even your mother would appreciate. Not only gave you a better figure but got rid of a lot of wrinkles.

Instead of gripin' you should be grateful, for Christ's sake!"

Those who really riled him, especially during depression years, came with only a yearning to become an entertainer. They'd invade the press car, or intercept him when he was arriving or leaving, and beg him to watch them perform and write a little story for the papers.

"Every goddamn one of 'em wants to be in center ring," Butler growled, "even if he can't do a damn thing more excitin' than wrestle a bear or pat a tiger on the rump.

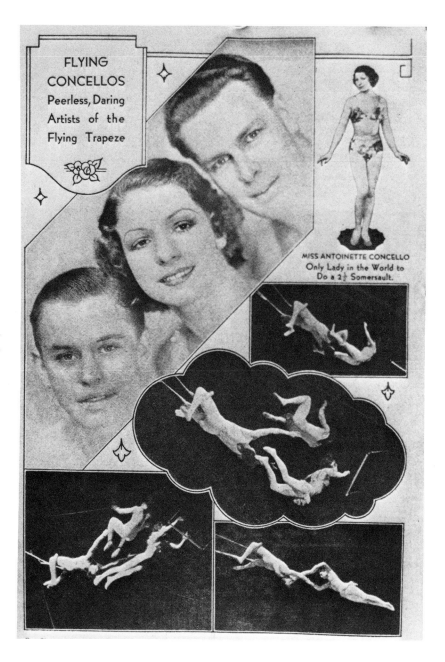

One of Butler's favorite promotions and thrilling acts was the Flying Concellos, headed by his good friend Arthur M. Concello and his wife, Antoinette, who performed the triple somersault.

The country is full of these pimps and tarts itchin' to perform. It's fiendish!

"Did I tell you about the old fellow who stayed on in winter quarters to help feed the animals and clean cages? The old faht took a likin' to Lotus, the big hippo. By spring he could pet the damn thing like a dog, and Lotus opened his mouth for Joe to pick straw out of his teeth.

"One day Joe told me he'd worked up a routine where he could stick his head in Lotus' mouth. Now wasn't that excitin' as hell? I told him go see Valdo, but I was his target. He got on somehow and was there when the show hit Philly.

"I ran into him there, and he wanted me to do a story. I told him I'd heard the show was droppin' his act; it was too dull. 'Goose it up,' I said to him. 'Put some life in it.'

"He said they couldn't drop it now, 'cause he'd mailed a thousand postal cards to friends in and around Scranton, his home town, tellin' them to come see his act. When I told him he might not last until Scranton, he whimpered like hell.

"Mr. Butler, he says, 'I put my head in Lotus' mouth up to my shoulders; the stink is awful. What more can I do?'

" 'You might stick your head up his a--,' I suggested.

" 'But Mr. Butler!' he says, blushin' like hell; he was really upset.

" 'Not with your glasses on, Joe!' I says. 'Take your glasses off!' I never had any more trouble with him, you bet."

Butler converted a couple of albino American Negroes into a profitable attraction for a season or two, after they had failed as a pair of Ecuadorean cannibals. It was a good example of psychology and promotion.

Dr. Richard W. Brislin, psychologist and circus aficionado at the Culture Learning Institute, East-West Center, Honolulu, Hawaii, said Butler was constantly thinking of ways to attract nationwide attention to the Big Show, preferably at no cost.

Writing in the *White Tops*, official publi-cation of the Circus Fans Association of America, for September-October 1980, Dr. Brislin stated:

"I doubt very much if Roland Butler could verbalize the phenomena of contrast effects sufficiently well to receive credit on an intro-psych exam, but that hardly matters.

"Circus people possess insights into well-established psychological principles and they use them very efficiently in organizing and selling their show."

Dr. Brislin cited the case of "two very special people" in the sideshow who were albino, often dressed like Neanderthal cavemen, and who had massive amounts of long hair protruding from their heads every which way.

Butler changed their names to Eko and Iko, dressed them stylishly, and billed them as "Ambassadors from Mars." About the time the circus opened in Madison Square Garden, he learned a national hair-dressers convention was to be held in a New York hotel. Somehow he managed to get tickets for Eko and Iko. They were seated on the front row, and photographers had been notified, of course.

When the president banged his gavel calling the convention to order, Eko and Iko stood up, doffed their big straw hats, and exposed great shocks of hair in front of hundreds of well-groomed and coifed hair stylists. Newspapers all around the country printed the picture.

The hairdressers jumped on Butler for what they considered a crude and tasteless joke, but he assured them Eko and Iko brought the organization nationwide publicity and said they should be grateful to him for putting their organization in the public eye.

"As a psychologist, I think of this story as a good example of contrast effects," Dr. Brislin wrote. "The impact of the performers from the Big Show is heightened because of the background against which they were seen.

John Ringling North, nephew of the five founding brothers who became circus president after his uncle John Ringling passed away in December, 1936.

"Another example is the aerialist, in center ring, who nonchalantly tosses his golden cape into the sawdust before climbing into the trapeze. This gesture is good showmanship since it happens against a background of pomp and spectacle.

"It is interesting to circus insiders to see the aerialist carefully brush off the $2,000 cape once he is back in the dressing room."

Dr. Brislin noted that the audience sees only the glamor of the circus, not the one-night stands, the constant worry about office receipts, and other problems.

"Since circus people are quite aware of the audience's tendency to see more glamor and exotica than is actually present," he wrote, "they arrange their acts to build upon the audience's point of view."

Brislin wrote that he was "manipulated" by Unus, an acrobat whose finale was to balance on a globe on one finger while twirling rings on wrists and ankles. Unus wore a glove believed to conceal a brace for his finger — Brislin was certain he re-moved the glove before his stand, when actually it was done afterward.

The psychologist said Unus's act was "selective perception," meaning people see what they want to see.

"Circus people know this," Brislin wrote, "and they are happy to arrange their acts so the positive benefits of selective perception are maximized."

Unus, a carpenter and cabinetmaker in Vienna before he became an entertainer, performed all over Europe and once was photographed standing on one finger on a cornice of a twenty-two story building — the tallest in Europe — before coming to America.

He began, he said, by placing his finger in a bottle and standing on it. Unus dressed in formal attire and used a cane in his performance. He retired to Sarasota, Florida, several years ago.

His act was no trick; it was balance, he says.

CHAPTER ELEVEN

OFTEN CALLED "Big Bertha" after the mammoth cannon the Germans aimed at France in World War I, and occasionally referred to as "The greatest, the grandest, and the goddamndest," the Ringling Bros and Barnum & Bailey Combined Circus was all that and more.

"Anybody who never saw the Big Show in those days doesn't have any idea what he missed," says Merle Evans, the band leader from 1919 through 1969. "We had everything. There was nothing we needed that wasn't right on the lot. They had a commissary wagon parked right beside the cookhouse. You could buy shoes, shirts, cigarettes, candy bars, tooth paste — even postage stamps.

"We had two barbers — regular barbers they were, and good at that; traveled with the show. Every morning they'd set up their chairs and have hot water for shaves. In those days every man got his shaves at the barber shop. We paid a quarter for a haircut.

"The show carried 125 cooks and waiters; baked all its pies and cakes, and served close to 4,000 meals a day. We even had our own blacksmith shop, light plant, hospital car — the whole works!"

Moving this tented city from coast to coast and border to border in the United States and into two Canadian provinces in every kind of weather was a tremendous task involving men, machines, elephant and horsepower — an example of logistics no towner could comprehend.

It was only 8 miles from Windsor, Ontario, to Detroit, but 718 from Portland, Oregon, to San Francisco. No matter, the move must be complete — every stake and pole, tent and line, horse and wagon, prop and performer.

The Big Show claimed it had eighty double-length steel railroad cars in its makeup, but Joe McKennon, veteran trouper and author of several circus books, says otherwise.

"The Ringling wagons were lighter and hauled much lighter loads, and for years their flatcars were much shorter than their smaller competitors," McKennon wrote in *Logistics of the American Circus.*

"In the seasons of 1929 and 1930, Sells-Floto on forty cars carried a big top very little smaller and a seating capacity almost equal to the Ringling show."

McKennon said the Ringling-Barnum show used 192 feet of flatcar space for big top poles and stakes, while Sells-Floto used only 56 feet.

Anyway, this was the makeup of the four trains used by the Ringling Bros and Barnum & Bailey Circus in its prime:

First section:

Preliminary essentials, including personnel and equipment of cookhouse and dining departments; layout, commissary, horseshoeing, harness-making, and blacksmith departments; timekeepers, animal men, menagerie tent, and cages of wild animals; giraffe dens, trucks, tractors, Caterpillars and drivers; colorful vehicles including spectacular floats; red, white, and yellow ticket wagons; tax wagon and office wagon.

Second section:

Big Top and sideshow tents, horse and wardrobe tents, canvas men, pole and stake wagons; personnel and equipment of property department, light and sanitation departments; two herds of working elephants and their handlers; truck and tractor drivers, motor fleet, diesel plants, four general admission seat wagons, concession wagons.

Third section:

Seven herds of performing elephants; horses, ponies, camels, and zebras; ring stock department men, including trainers, hostlers, and grooms; elephant men, animal trainers, and seat department personnel. Also thirty-nine wagons, including twenty-four steel-seat wagons; band wagon, wardrobe wagon, stage coach, and tally ho.

Fourth section:

Big Show and sideshow performers, band men, staff members, executives, and office personnel. The fourth section generally was made up of staterooms and Pullman sleepers.

Loading and departure schedules went like this:

First section: Begins to load at approximately 5:30 P.M. Usually loaded and ready to leave for the next stand at 10:30 P.M.

Second section: Ordinarily loaded and ready to leave at 2 A.M.

Third section: Always loaded as soon as the first section pulls out, but does not leave until second section is on its way.

Fourth section: Ready to leave any time after the third section departs.

First meal served at the next stand was breakfast, no matter the time of day. It was quite substantial and satisfying and included cereal, fresh fruit or juices; bacon, ham, or sausage; hot cakes, eggs, baking powder biscuits, French toast, boiled or fried potatoes, and coffee, tea, or milk. Potatoes in one form or another were served at every meal.

One trouper happily recalled that when he joined up, "They even had pork chops for breakfast!"

Two of the Big Show's cookhouse superintendents well remembered were George Blood and John Staley.

When breakfast was over, waiters began setting up for lunch. Suppertime was usually from 3:30 to 5 o'clock.

Best meal of the year was Fourth of July dinner, with turkey, fruit, nuts, and all the trimmings, even patriotic decorations. This usually was served in a different city each year — Springfield or Fitchburg, Massachusetts; Utica, Buffalo or Rochester, New York; Pittsburgh or Bradford, Pennsylvania, or perhaps Montreal, Quebec, or Kitchener, Ontario.

Roland Butler was at his best in the old press car, entertaining writers. If he didn't have a new story after a season on the road, he'd add a new twist to an old one or express his feelings on topics of the time. He liked to perform:

"Watch this," he'd say when a couple he knew drove in and parked as close to the press car as possible. "This tight old bastard won't even take his wife to the movies — drives out here at least once a week for their entertainment. I'll entertain 'em, by God!"

With that he'd open a window facing the parking lot and begin with a blasphemous declaration, such as:

"We've got to get some air in this g--d--- oven; it must be better than a hundred degrees in here — hotter than a farmer's outhouse in Iowa in August!

"Say, Frank; didn't you run into more damn skinflints last season than ever? I did, Jim to Mollie. They swarmed at me from every angle, wantin' passes to the whole damn lot — press cards, they wanted — or tryin' to wangle a meal in the cookhouse. It was fiendish!

"And you know, I know a lot of tightwads right here in Sarasota, Jim to Mollie. They come to me wantin' old wagon wheels, bull hooks, costumes — anything. And they wouldn't pay a quarter to see John Ringling parade down Main Street in his drawers!"

Butler was acting now, not alone for guests in the car but for the couple outside. He paced up and down the aisle, flinging his arms, raising his voice, frequently glancing toward the couple to see their reaction, and enjoying every minute.

"I asked one old faht the other day if he'd ever been to the art museum," Butler boomed. " 'No,' he says, 'I never got a pass.' Can you imagine? He never got a

pass! I reckon the old miser expected an engraved invitation. Ten million dollars worth of art out there, and he never got a pass! You run into 'em everywhere; thick as tarts. Haw, haw, haw!"

He was referring to the John and Mable Ringling Museum of Art on the opposite side of town, opened in conjunction with the Ringling School of Art and Junior College on October 1, 1931.

"Oh, did I tell you about the fella tried to sell us a picture of Mr. Ringling? Sat'day, I think it was. It was a real monstrosity, by

One year Butler was called on to promote this child prodigy, Mister Mistin. Despite his feelings, Butler did his usual thorough job, and was relieved when the act lasted only one season.

God. Looked like a daguerreotype o' Christ!"

Then Butler verbally spanked all amateur artists, claiming they hounded him to buy paintings of circus characters done by people with no more talent than a billy goat.

"I told one of 'em I could do a better job with a toothbrush stuck up my ---," he shouted as the car pulled away, the woman with hands cupped over her ears and her husband laughing fit to kill.

"Don't worry," Butler assured his audience. "They'll be back next week for another installment. Happens all the time."

During the winter young bucks from the circus made extra money boxing on weekly programs in the American Legion coliseum every Monday night. John Ringling liked that.

Ringling had a box at ringside, seldom missed a fight if he was in town, and made small wagers. He attended championship fights all over the country, usually as guest of his friend, promoter Tex Rickard.

At home Roland and Estelle seldom went out at night but were early risers. He followed fight results in the local papers, searching for angles he might use in a story or cartoon.

He pounced on any incident or idea, expanded it to make an appealing feature, or filed it away in memory. One of his gems while the show was in winter quarters involved a mangy old lion named Brutus, an ill, aged, and bony specimen that might not survive the winter.

Someone in the circus hierarchy, perhaps Henry Ringling ("Buddy") North or the vet, suggested that Brutus be put to sleep because he no longer was an asset but a hospital case. Word reached Roland that Brutus may have received a broken jaw in a fight with another lion and it might make a good local story.

"Good little local story!" Butler thundered. "It'll make a terrific story that'll make all the papers. The wire services will

go for it, too. Just let us handle it, for Christ's sake!"

He telephoned a struggling young dentist new in town and told him the vet needed help in repairing a broken jaw and replacing a few teeth for Brutus, a sick old lion. Brutus was too ill to resist, he added, so there would be no danger. It would be easy to wire up the jaw, and the operation could bring valuable publicity to a man just starting in his profession.

Butler notified the press that this experiment in bestial dentistry would occur at a certain hour next day. He apologized for such short notice but explained Brutus appeared to be in great pain and must be treated as soon as possible.

Reporters came from as far away as Tampa. Wire services asked for coverage. Winter quarters bristled with activity that day.

While the dentist stood at the ready in white jacket, clutching forceps and fine wire, the veterinarian pumped ether into old Brutus like putting air into a bicycle tire.

When Brutus finally closed his eyes and fell into a stupor, the dentist and vet gave a fine exhibition of cooperation in dental surgery — snipping, inserting, adjusting, and stitching — pausing to discuss the procedure in low voices. When it was all over, Brutus was whisked off to the hospital tent.

"You fellows check with me tomorrow; we'll have a full report," Butler promised reporters. "By God, this'll make dental history. Never before, far as we know, has a wild beast survived an operation such as this, and at his age. It's phenomenal!"

"How's Brutus?" local reporters asked next morning when they called at Butler's office. Others telephoned to inquire.

"How is he?" Butler replied with a roar and a look of surprise. "Why, he's fine. They tell us the operation was a success. I guess his jaw is still a bit sore but he'll be all right. Let's go see."

He put on his hat and led the way to a

cage in the big house. Three lions were padding about in a large cage while one lay dozing in a smaller enclosure. It was unusually quiet, and there were no keepers about.

"There he is!" Butler shouted, pointing to the small cage. "That's old Brutus; he's all right. This is fantastic. The whole world of dentistry will be amazed at this scientific achievement, by God! We've written a whole new chapter in dental history among the wild beasts."

What Butler didn't tell was that Brutus never awakened.

Butler was much impressed when he dropped in to visit his friend, Lou DeFour, veteran sideshow manager then at Chicago's Century of Progress exposition in 1933. DeFour was dressed as an explorer, with pith helment and snake boots, carrying a whip and pistol.

He had gone all out with thatched hut and tropical shrubbery, displaying what he called "Natives direct from the heart of darkest Africa." Actually, they were Chicago blacks of assorted sizes, displaying considerable portions of bare skin.

"Every morning I go down to the waterfront and hire them for a dollar a day," DeFour told Butler. "They peel off and get right into the spirit of things."

"Great show!" Butler said. "It gave an exciting impression of the Dark Continent, by God! After all, who th' hell knew the difference?"

CHAPTER TWELVE

JOHN RINGLING was in bad shape both physically and financially in the mid 1930s. He was suing for a divorce from Emily and suffering from the gout, his many developments in the Sarasota area lay dormant, and his once warm friendship with Sam Gumpertz had soured.

Ringling appeared at the office in Madison Square Garden about the time the 1936 edition was to open, accompanied by his nephew, John Ringling North, and his nurse, Ina Sanders.

He claimed the circus was badly managed and called the circus paper the worst he'd ever seen. A violent argument developed, and Gumpertz ordered him to leave. Ringling emerged a bitter, dejected old man.

Later that season he met Roland Butler by chance one day when he appeared on the lot to borrow money from Carl Hathaway, an old friend. He tore into Butler about Mrs. Edith Ringling, widow of Charles, who held a third interest in the circus.

"What do you mean puttin' out that story about Mrs. Charlie being 'Mother of the circus,' Roland?" he whined. "You know better than to spread such crap. Circus mother my eye!"

Butler bristled but managed to keep his calm, realizing Ringling was not his boss but might eventually gain control.

"Mr. Ringling, we didn't put that out," Butler replied. "The newspapers in Chicago broke the story. They got it from outside sources without any help from anybody in the press department, and the wire services picked it up. I'll swear to that."

"Roland!" Ringling's ruddy face turned a deeper red. "You know damn well there are plenty of bastards already full of that propaganda without our press department feedin' them more. I don't want to read any such crap again. I won't stand for it. You understand?"

"I understand, Mr. Ringling," Butler conceded, and walked away.

When the circus ended its tour in Tampa on November 11, 1936, and went into winter quarters next day, John Ringling was in his mansion, Ca d' Zan. There he ate and drank with his friend, Fred Bradna, equestrian director, who briefed him on circus matters.

Bradna, a fellow Alsatian, wrote that he enjoyed John Ringling's confidence not only when he was the multimillionaire nabob of circusdom but in the last cruel days when, "with scarcely a dime in his pocket, diabetes in his system, emptiness in his heart, and a body wasted from a thrombosis, he really needed friendship."

Ten days later Ringling left for New York aboard the Jomar, after telling friends he hoped to raise enough to pay off his two notes, regain control of the circus, and "kick the thievin' bastards out."

Instead;, he fell ill and quickly developed bronchial pneumonia. Early on the morning of December 2 John Ringling died. Six months past his seventieth birthday, he'd lived longer than any of his brothers and gained more worldly possessions than all the rest combined.

There was genuine sorrow among many who had trouped with the Ringlings and had hoped that somehow the circus might go back under family control. Among them was Roland Butler, who had no love for him as a man but admittedly admired his achievements as a promoter and manipulator.

Ringling's will provided $5,000 annually for his sister, Ida Ringling North, and named her and her sons, John Ringling North and Henry Ringling North, as trustees of the estate, appraised at $22,366,000.

It included the art museum and home next door; acres of beach property on Bird, St. Armand's, Lido, and Longboat keys; oil wells, railroads, ranchlands, and business property. His one-third interest in Ringling Bros and Barnum & Bailey Circus was valued at $650,000 and other circus properties — most of them inactive at the time — at $616,000.

John Ringling North was executor of his uncle's estate. He scraped up $850,000 to settle tax claims of $3,753,138, made other deals, and acquired seventy shares of circus stock at a bankrupt sale.

North now controlled 370 shares of the 1,000 outstanding. His aunt, Edith Ringling, and his cousin by marriage, Aubrey Ringling, voted their shares with him, and when the directors met in the spring of 1937 they elected North president of the circus and his brother, Henry, vice president and assistant to the president, for five-year terms effective at the end of the season.

The tour was one of the worst in many years. Organized labor hounded Gumpetz, and in May he signed a contract for five years that doubled the pay of workingmen from thirty to sixty dollars a month and keep while on the road.

Butler and his press department managed to survive all this, while most executives and performers were jittery throughout the season. Rumors kept the circus "backyard" in turmoil.

Dexter Fellows, the popular old press agent, fell ill that summer, and many on the show expressed concern.

"Poor old Dex," Butler mourned to newsmen, "lyin' up in that hospital in Hattiesburg, Mississippi, in horrible shape. I'm afraid there's not much hope for him."

"What's the matter with Dexter?" a reporter asked. Butler repeated the question as if everybody knew, then shouted, "He can't piss!

"Poor old fellow; there's nobody with him but Signe [his wife], and she can't do a goddamn thing; she's absolutely helpless! I wish to hell one of us could go see him, but there's no chance. It wouldn't make any difference now; he's too far gone.

"It'll be a big loss to all of us on the show. Dexter was tops in his field; unquestionably. All the newspaper folks knew and liked the old guy. He was experienced and colorful, I'll say that."

Bill Ballentine, clown, publicist, and headmaster of Clown College for years, once wrote a book in which he called Fellows "The fabulous sawdust press agent." In the same volume he referred to Butler as "That lovable, snorting war-horse of the circus."

The show ended the 1937 tour in Miami on November 9 and went into winter quarters next day — the earliest since 1934. Sam Gumpertz was out.

The North brothers assumed command and named Arthur M. Concello, star of the flying trapeze and triple somersault man, general manager of the show. Concello proved to be a cagey and capable operator, generally popular with most employees and inventive in the mold of James A. Bailey.

The press department remained unchanged except for the departed Fellows. Butler and Braden carried on with the help of others.

The circus was still reeling from the

Great Depression and the internal dissension during Gumpertz's regime. Charges of mismanagement were in the courts, and family squabbles broke out. These, of course, were embarrassing for the press department and generally ignored, but newspapers and wire services covered them adequately.

His first move stamped John Ringling North as a worthy successor to his uncles as a promoter. The two North brothers called on Mrs. Gertrude Davies Lintz at her home in Brooklyn one night early in December and agreed to buy her pet gorilla and two chimpanzees for $10,000.

The circus had not exhibited a gorilla in many years, and little was known about these great anthropoid apes from equatorial Africa. Circus patrons need never be told this gorilla had been raised in Brooklyn and called "Buddha" or "Buddy" for seven years.

His coarse black hair, ample frame, and long arms made him impressive, and an ugly scar on the side of his mouth left some teeth exposed, giving him a permanent sneer and a mean, threatening look.

Butler welcomed the opportunity to make a contribution to the public knowledge of gorillas. He saw "Buddy" as "The mightiest monster ever captured by man," "The most fiendishly ferocious brute that breathes," and "The world's most terrifying living creature."

The gorilla had reached winter quarters after being sneaked aboard a passenger train from New York. It was Sunday afternoon, and the big wooden crate housing "Buddy" was hustled out to quarters aboard a truck.

"Come in!" Butler bellowed when reporters called on him next morning. He reached for his hat and announced: "We'll go right out and see the gorilla. He's a pip!"

The confused ape sat huddled in the corner of a deer cage, peeling and eating a banana. An old army blanket was draped about his shoulders to keep out the morning chill.

"By God, Mr. Kroener; he's a frightful lookin' beast," the press agent said to Richard Kroener, the keeper. "I can see he's a very mean animal."

"He's nice fellow, Mr. Butler," Kroener replied in his soft German accent, smiling tolerantly. "He's very gentle."

"Gentle!" Butler roard. "Why he's the most terrifying beast I ever laid eyes on; he's a real monster if I ever saw one."

Circus jargon, especially in the Roland Butler tone, was new to Kroener, who'd been the gorilla's companion for the seven years since the animal arrived from Africa as an injured and frightened orphan eighteen months old and weighing twenty-two pounds.

"I tell you what we've got to do, Mr. Kroener," Butler said, already busy hatching ideas to promote the latest circus attraction. "Make him mean; feed him raw meat. Get him a tire to cut his teeth on — a damn big truck tire. By God, has he got any teeth?"

"Yes, Mr. Butler; his teeth like human's."

The gorilla, half the banana still in his hairy, upraised hand, turned his gaze toward Butler. He blinked his sparkling brown eyes at the half dozen spectators gathered at his steel-barred prison and let out a low, grasping grunt like a boar looking for acorns.

"Well, he's gonna be all right," Butler noted. "We'll make him the meanest son of a bitch the world has ever seen!"

When Butler learned from Kroener the gorilla's name was "Buddha" and he was called "Buddy," the press agent thundered disapproval.

"Christ Almighty! What a horrible name for a terrifying gorilla. Everybody on the show knows Henry Ringling North as 'Buddy.' We sure as hell can't have the vice president of the show and a gorilla wearin' the same name. Buddy! Humpf. We'll take care of that first thing."

The Butlers' daughter, Estelle, shown on her favorite mount, "Light of Asia," was beautiful, talented and regarded by many as one of the best performers on the show. This picture was taken in 1942.

Buddy North, one of Butler's friends and admirers, took a personal interest in the gorilla. He chose the name "Gargantua" from the hero in *Gargantua and Pantagruel*, a satirical romance by François Rabelais, which North had read while a student at Yale. Butler added "the Great."

As Butler saw it, the gorilla was a "natural" because so little was known about these apes. This specimen had almost reached maturity, weighing over 300 pounds. His dark, shaggy coat sprinkled with silver added to his bulky appearance; the sneer enhanced it.

Butler liked the name "Gargantua" and felt it his responsibility to make it return the purchase price many times over. The exact figure was never mentioned by any circus employee, and John Ringling North would only say, "He's worth $100,000."

Butler began his promotion by emphasizing the gorilla's great size and strength, commencing a "teaser" campaign with bills reading only, "The terror is coming!"

First billing matter showed Gargantua the Great smashing through tall grass, weeds and palmettoes, mouth open in a blood-curdling scream, teeth like spikes, and lips dripping gore. Butler the artist accentuated the sneer — caused by a dash of nitric acid flung by a disgruntled sailor at the time the baby ape arrived in America.

In the massive right hand, raised high over the shoulder, was what appeared to be the body of a tribal chief one-tenth the size of his captor, and in the background was a gang of natives charging through the jungle armed with shields, spears, and blowguns.

This artistic production in vivid color was splashed on billboards with text describing Gargantua the Great as "The largest gorilla ever exhibited," and "The world's most terrifying living creature."

Butler claimed tests showed Gargantua had the strength of twenty-seven men. While his special steel and glass, air-conditioned cage was being built, the gorilla was confined in a deer cage. One day Butler told the press John Ringling North had inadvertantly stepped too close and Gargantua had grabbed his arm and clawed it, inflicting a terrible wound.

The circus president was rushed to a hospital, Butler reported, where a record dose of antitoxin was injected, adding that if North had not been wearing a leather jacket his arm might have been severed.

Butler soon realized he might have gone a bit too far with the vicious angle and tempered it by emphasizing that Gargantua the Great was confined to a specially built, escape-proof cage of double-thick glass and chilled steel bars to safeguard the public.

He also said John North had issued orders to shoot the gorilla on sight if by any chance he was ever seen outside his cage.

Gargantua the Great's picture appeared in newspapers and magazines around the world, in news stories and advertisements. His likeness was spread on five million lithograph sheets, window cards, heralds, programs, billboards, and other circus literature, according to Butler's estimate.

Butler changed the billing each season, from "The world's most terrifying living creature," or "The mightiest monster ever captured by man," to "The most fiendishly ferocious brute that breathes."

Gargantua did nothing but focus his limpid brown eyes on a constant stream of customers, yet he became the most widely known and profitable circus animal since P. T. Barnum's Jumbo more than fifty years before. Gargantua was truly the "Circus Star of the Century."

The circus couldn't finish its 1938 tour even with the help of Gargantua. The New York opening was marred by labor trouble. The pay scale that prevailed in winter quarters continued through the New York and Boston engagements, but this time union leaders demanded full pay immediately.

John North told them to "go to hell," and so many walked out it left only management, performers, and animals. The spec featured Frank ("Bring 'Em Back Alive")

Buck as the maharajah of Nepal and his court, but instead of a glittering pageant with Buck riding an elephant, he came in walking, with a pet cheetah on his arm.

Circus officials and performers, aided by many from the audience, made a program possible, but the strike lasted through the next day, then settlement was reached to finish out the New York and Boston dates.

There was sporadic labor trouble when the show returned to Brooklyn and in Washington, but it moved on to Baltimore, Philadelphia, and Newark in the face of dwindling business.

It had engagements in Trenton, Wilmington, Reading, Harrisburg, Pittsburgh, Wheeling, Columbus, Dayton, Lima, Sandusky, Fort Wayne, Toledo, Erie, Buffalo, Rochester, Watertown, Syracuse, and Binghamton.

North claimed the show was losing $40,000 a week and that he couldn't meet salary demands. Organized labor continued to picket and boycott. North gave notice of a 25 percent cut in pay for everybody.

The circus made it to Scranton, Pennsylvania, on June 22, but there was no show. Pickets surrounded the lot, water was shut off, and there was no food or ice.

The mayor of Scranton supported the pickets and told the circus to get out of town. When North asked him how, he answered, "That's not my problem, son."

After two tense days and nights, the circus limped off to Sarasota winter quarters, licking its wounds. Performers had voted not to join the strike.

"A circus can make money faster and lose it quicker than anything else I know," Merle Evans observed, and it's true.

Garantua the Great and a few other attractions, some selected acts, Merle Evans and his band, along with a trainload of equipment, joined the Al G. Barnes–Sells-Floto Circus, part of the Ringling combine, at Redfield, South Dakota, giving its first performance on July 11.

It was billed as "Al G. Barnes and Sells-Floto Circus presenting Ringling Bros and Barnum & Bailey stupendous new features."

Gargantua's box office appeal exceeded expectations at almost every stop. Evans recalls groups of people wandering about the lot, inquiring, "Where's that thing they call 'Guarantee'?" They stood in line in broiling sun, numbing cold, and drenching rain to peek at the gorilla.

The circus did not return to winter quarters until November 22, and North informed stockholders the show made $400,000 that season instead of showing a loss.

CHAPTER THIRTEEN

THE SEASON'S EVENTS were a tremendous handicap to Butler and his press department, but they weathered the storm and kept the circus in the public eye whenever possible, always emphasizing the good.

Butler arranged for memorial services honoring C. E. Walters and Charles Smith at Wahpeton, North Dakota, on Sunday, August 14, complete with a minister and Merle Evans and his band.

Walters and Smith were killed when lightning struck a center pole while Ringling Bro's Circus was setting up at Wahpeton on June 10, 1897, and are buried there. It made a nice little story for Midwest newspapers.

The Butlers also visited the cemetery in Baraboo, Wisconsin, where many members of the Ringling family are buried, among them papa August and mother Salome.

John Ringling's death had brought sharp division in the family, with the Norths on one side — called the 51s because they now controlled 51 percent of the circus stock. Others held 49 percent and, of course, were known as the 49ers.

Charges of mismanagement followed the Gumpertz regime and continued after North took over. There were many suits and countersuits among the heirs. Interviewed aboard her private Pullman, the Caledonia, Mrs. Edith Ringling told reporters:

"If John Ringling had spent his whole life trying to mess up his affairs, and hired two Philadelphia lawyers to help him, he couldn't have done a better job!"

The circus badly needed a transfusion following the Gumpertz regime, and the Norths and their right-hand man, Concello, provided it.

John Ringling North — thirty-four when he assumed command — adopted the lifestyle of his aberrant old uncle John, even to living aboard the Jomar, where he had a valet, maid, and chef. The plush old Pullman had a pantry and bar, both well-stocked. North often told reporters he had a weight problem.

He usually lay a-bed until noon and stayed up most of the night, as his uncle had done. If he was in Sarasota, he might appear at winter quarters dressed in the finest toggery, even to riding boots, gloves, and a crop.

Choosing one of his favorite horses, he'd canter over the grounds for half an hour or more, then drop in at the business office or perhaps pay a call on the press car.

At night he often could be found in the plush John Ringling Hotel, where ambitious youngsters and some not so young tried out for jobs as aerialists, tumblers, wire walkers, or clowns. Sometimes these exhibitions uncovered talent, sometimes not, but they always turned a profit because the public was invited to watch, for a fee.

North cultivated friendships in high places, as did his uncle John, but he went a notch higher. He is listed in biographical tomes as a showman and circus producer or

Toward the end of his career, Roland Butler was pictured outside the old press car. Although wrinkles line his face, he is still the old war horse, full of determination.

an entrepreneur, a distinction none of his uncles achieved. Oddly, biographers ignored them.

North also was a musician and composed several numbers featured in the circus. A close friend of Prince Rainier of Monaco, North often served as a judge for the international circus competition held annually in Monaco.

North's right-hand man was Concello, a thinking fellow who installed many innovations and improved the whole operation. He designed special steel grandstand seats that could be quickly set up or packed away for movement to the next town.

Concello was quick to spot any waste or inefficiency, knew every facet of the gigantic operation, and saved Johnny North a million headaches.

Every seven years North would go into one of his moods, have a violent argument with Concello, and fire him. Soon they would become reconciled, and Concello would go back on the job as general manager and serve for another seven years.

Concello now lives in retirement, but every knowledgeable circus person will agree he was the smartest operator since James A. Bailey.

North retained James A. Haley, who had been John Ringling's accountant, to handle paperwork on the estate and put the tangled affairs in some sort of order.

There were federal, state, county, and city taxes amounting to some $13.5 million, but no government wanted to take over a circus. Years earlier the federal government had seized a circus for taxes and had soon learned that a circus was not always an asset.

North and his attorneys were in and out of court for years, fighting claims and working out deals wherever possible. Even Emily's divorce case against John Ringling and his estate wasn't settled until 1943 — seven years after he died.

"The Ringling estate was the most involved I ever heard of, and it is a delicate situation," Florida's Secretary of State Robert A. Gray said. "There are many suits pending and there have been numerous differences. We have had a series of attorneys in this case."

North wanted the state to take over the art museum, but the city of Sarasota also wanted it. The same was true of the ornate residence. North likewise wanted to settle the estate and get what he could.

The circus, and particularly its press department, suffered through all these maneuvers, which continued until February 9, 1946, when the state of Florida took over the mansion of John and Mable Ringling and the John and Mable Ringling Museum of Art next door.

When it was over North held 30 percent of the circus stock, in addition to oil wells in Oklahoma and Texas, part interest in the Ringling Theater in Baraboo, the Pullman car Jomar, John Ringling Hotel, the Whitaker house on Bird Key where Harding was supposed to visit, and half the silver and china in the Ringling residence, Ca d' Zan.

Henry Ringling ("Buddy") North, six years younger than his brother John, proved a crutch for the press department. Angular and taller than John, the Yale graduate had much the personality of his uncle Charlie, made friends easily, and was quite popular with personnel at all levels because he knew and understood their problems.

He dressed fashionably but spent most of his time at winter quarters or with the circus when it was on tour. He usually contributed a feature story to the circus's route book, at Butler's urging.

The dusty, musty, old press car was completely renovated through Butler's friendship with Henry North, a bit of ingenuity, and a wheel of moldy cheese.

"The place was in terrible shape," Butler related. "The cheese was a great big goddamn thing — smelled like hell. Some fellow sent it to me from upstate New York by

When it was quiet in winter quarters, Butler thought up such features as the Ringling mustache cups, pictured with their owners. The photograph was widely circulated and brought much publicity. It appeared in the old *Life* magazine.

express. It had been on the road a week or more before it got to us.

"I was busy and shoved the damn thing under the table; actually forgot about it a week or two. By then heat and humidity had worked on it, and it was really ripe, if you know what I mean.

"One day Buddy was over to look at some art work, and when he leaned over the stink hit him. You could almost feel it, by God. He staggered back on his heels and said, 'Hunh! What's that I smell?'

" 'Rats! The place is overrun with 'em,' I says. 'We put out rat poison, and they eat it and crawl up into the ceilin' to die. It ain't healthy. This place is a pigsty and dangerous to us working folks. We could come down with some dreadful disease. Don't you agree, Buddy?' "

Next morning carpenters came in and commenced a complete overhaul. And what happened to the cheese?

"I took it home, but Stelle wouldn't have it in the house. I had to bury it in the backyard — deep, so it wouldn't smell up the neighborhood."

Butler never liked Sam Gumpertz. Although he worked for the myopic little man during the five years he ran the show, the press agent's feelings congealed into what amounted to hatred and distrust.

It may have originated with an interview published in the *Billboard* of March 25, 1933, in which Gumpertz as executive vice president of the circus rated his press agents on ability. He named Dexter Fellows first, Frank Braden second, and Roland Butler third.

Not until August 15, 1938, did Butler explode in an "open letter" of about two thousand words. Written from Omaha, Nebraska, it began:

"A clipping has been forwarded to me, cut from the July issue of the *Reporter* published by the American Federation of Actors, reproducing a letter you sent to Mr. Ralph Whitehead, executive secretary of the organization, claiming that the A.F.A. benefited the Ringling Bros and Barnum & Bailey Circus last season.

"I have been expecting that sooner or later you would belch forth with some such endorsement of your old buddy, Ralph Whitehead, for you and Whitehead have many things in common, and with the exception of Whitehead outranking you in intelligence, you two cronies are as alike as two peas in a pod.

"You have both set out to destroy the circus, you're both poison to the cause of organized labor, and you are both thoroughly detested by the millions of decent people who love 'The Greatest Show on Earth,' including the multitude of staunch true friends of the circus among the Jewish people, who are ashamed to own you and Whitehead as members of their race.

"More than a quarter of a century of conniving crystallized early last summer when you sold out the Big Show and the Big Show's people to Whitehead. It was nearly

thirty years ago that you really laid the foundation for that job."

Butler claimed that when the Ringlings became unquestioned leaders of the circus world, Gumpertz decided the time was ripe to cultivate them, "which you did with a vengeance."

"Posing as a friend," Butler wrote, "you barnacled on to the circus when you were a representative of side show freaks. You stuck your nose into about everything that didn't concern you, offered all kinds of fool advice that wasn't welcome or accepted, and, refusing to be insulted, held to your lofty purpose of eventually taking the Ringlings for a ride."

Butler said the five-paragraph letter Gumpertz sent to Whitehead reprinted on the front page of the *Reporter* was a typical Gumpertz communication, "packed with deliberate downright lies."

"Whitehead wanted that kind of letter from you and he got it. The Ringling press department is not surprised at your reckless disregard for the truth. We had five years of you with the show and know that when it comes to high-powered lying, you make Ananais look like a piker."

Butler commented that after the agreement with the American Federation of Actors went into effect on June 1, 1937, it was impossible to hold workingmen, and changes in the working departments of the show took place on a more gigantic scale than at any time in circus history.

He claimed that 2,700 men came and went between June and November 1937 and that one department that had averaged six changes of men per season for more than 20 years had 42 during the 1937 summer.

"The cracks you make," Roland asserted, "about the equipment being well taken care of and in perfect shape at the end of the 1937 season due to loyalty of the men stamp you as an unscrupulous fabulist of the foulest type.

"When you set out to destroy the tents,

wagons, trucks and costly mechanical equipment of the show during the 1937 tour," Butler wrote, "after learning that the circus skids were under you and that the Ringlings were about to degumpertz the organization, you not only seriously damaged the prestige of the circus, but you handed organized labor a wallop below the belt."

Butler accused Gumpertz of "deliberate destruction" by failing to order necessary repair work done, and he claimed this cost the Ringlings "almost $100,000."

He said that in the second half of 1937 the show's physical property was so badly run down that the circus could no longer be photographed in its entirety for publicity purposes and that "the press department implored you to do something about the matter."

Tents were ripped and torn, Butler added, and the situation was "most difficult to explain to the press." He said there was daily talk about the circus looking as if it were on its last legs, and that "such a display of circus wreckage . . . failed to impress you.

"When told that the reputation of the Ringling Circus was being immeasurably injured by such a disgraceful condition, you said 'To hell with the Ringlings, I'll leave them a 'setup' that will cost so much it will force them out of business.' "

Butler's letter continued:

"During the five years you held forth around the circus in the capacity of front man for the New York Investors, mortgagees, drawing a salary of $25,000 per year and bearing the title of General Manager and Vice-President, your extreme incompetence gave the press agents more grief than they would have had in a life time of work under the direction of a real showman who knew what it was all about.

"The press agents felt from the beginning that you sold out the show to A.F.A. to increase the circus overhead, reduce profits and make mortgage lifting impossible. . . .

"When the circus got rid of you by paying the mortgage . . . the joy of the press agents knew no bounds."

The letter concluded by stating that if Gumpertz had written about conditions to Whitehead it would never have been printed or "embarrassed the great American Federation of Labor," and added that "A contemptible old renegade of your years . . . ought to be making peace with God."

Addressed to Gumpertz in his job then as manager of Hamid's Million Dollar Pier in Atlantic City, New Jersey, Butler signed the letter as general press representative of the circus and "Member of Theatrical Managers, Agents and Treasurers Union, No. 18032, A.F. of L."

Butler never received a reply, and none was expected.

One thing that seemed to send Roland Butler's blood pressure soaring was the circus title. Some considered it one of his little idiosyncracies, but to him it was anathema. He insisted that no period belonged after the "Bros" and that it should read "Ringling Bros and Barnum & Bailey Combined Circus."

A poster of 1900 vintage featuring the five founders' faces bore the title "Ringling Bro's," which wasn't a misplaced comma but an apostrophe indicating the possessive.

Many smaller circuses such as Christy Bros., Cole Bros., King Bros., Miller Bros., and Hoxie Bros. were not necessarily owned or operated by brothers. The title was used for effect — perhaps inspired by the Sells, Ringlings, and Gollmars, who really were brothers. The word "Bros." indicated size and stability.

Butler steadfastly insisted that the period did not belong after "Bros" in the Ringling title, and when it appeared he would go into a frenzy.

"Goddamn it!" he'd shout, his face reddening and his arms thrashing the air in frustration. "There's that pesky period again. Now, who in th' hell put it there? It's got to come out, for Christ's sake. Those pig-headed printers know it does not belong in there, but it always creeps in somehow. Christ Almighty!"

He would reach for the telephone and try to track down the culprit, fuming and cussing all the while.

Even now, if posters and window cards in collectors' hands bear a period after the word "Bros" in the circus title, rest assured they are not from the Butler era.

Butler compiled what he called "The Magazine of Wonders" for the 1938 season. It was a sixteen-page courier in two-color rotogravure, packed with pictures and text covering every phase of the circus. It was intended for use by the press only and was not for sale.

Used only during the brief season that ended June 22 in Scranton, it quickly disappeared. Roland reported that before the circus reached winter quarters more than a million copies of this informative little publication had been destroyed. A few years later, copies he had put aside were gobbled up by collectors at $3 each.

"I wish I'd kept a few thousand of the damn things," Butler grumbled. "I could have sold ten thousand of 'em, for Christ's sake."

All the paper had to be changed when the Ringling show finished out the season as part of the Al G. Barnes–Sells-Floto Circus.

CHAPTER FOURTEEN

GARGANTUA THE GREAT was a good drawing card for a couple of seasons, but by 1940 his popularity had begun to wane. Circus officials took note of such things, like merchants check on their stock.

After all, the hairy old ape did nothing more exciting than snuggle in a corner of his cage, squat on a stout wooden bench, or swing on a tire suspended from the ceiling by a heavy chain. The public always expected something new and exciting at the circus.

Performers and workingmen began calling the ape "Gargy," implying a certain familiarity if not affection, contrary to the image Butler had created.

John Ringling North learned of a gorilla named Toto owned by Mrs. Marie Hoyt, a wealthy widow living in Havana, Cuba. She and her husband, Kenneth, had captured Toto on safari in the French Congo in 1932 and had raised her from a baby. Mrs. Hoyt wouldn't sell her pet but made a lease agreement that gave her unlimited visiting privileges and provided that Jose Tomas, a kindly gentleman who had been the gorilla's keeper, go with Toto.

Mrs. Hoyt had tea with her pet every afternoon and often read poetry to her. The ape liked to cuddle a black and white kitten named Principe.

Tomas taught Toto to make letters with a pencil, draw with crayons, and play chess. He would take the gorilla for piggyback rides around the grounds of the Hoyt home. "Toto was always gentle and never caged in Cuba," Tomas said. "I taught her to count on fingers and toes; she would throw me kisses. Toto loved for people to come look at her. Gargantua never liked people — only maybe Mrs. Lintz, who raised him. He was sneaky and could be mean."

Toto, accompanied by Tomas and housed in an air-conditioned cage built for her and sent to Havana, arrived at Fort Lauderdale by boat and crossed the state by train.

The "gorilla wedding" was the main event of the season in winter quarters. Toto arrived in Florida on February 20, and the nuptials were scheduled two days later — on a Saturday and Washington's birthday. This was always a slow news day, which meant that Sunday papers would give the story space.

Two score reporters and photographers from around the state were there, including wire service representatives, to await the noon ceremony.

"We've had to postpone it a little while," Butler announced. "But you fellows stick around; you'll see the damndest thing you ever laid eyes on, the first gorilla weddin' in history. We'll pull it off if we have to blindfold and hog-tie the old lady."

He referred to Mrs. Hoyt, who'd gone into town to buy flowers and candy for Toto. She had told reporters there would be no wedding; that Toto was tired and upset from the voyage and needed rest.

Reporters were getting restless, and it was near 2 o'clock when tractors began shoving the two cages end to end. Someone put on a recording of Lohengrin's "Processional" and turned up the volume so it drowned out the noises coming from pens, cages, and pastures in winter quarters.

Glass panels at adjoining ends of the cages were removed so the gorillas could see, smell, and touch each other. Gargantua offered Toto some celery and then some lettuce, but she refused it. The two seemed more interested in what went on outside than inside their cages, watching as photographers worked with cameras and flash guns.

Gargantua grunted a few times and bounded around in his cage, but Toto didn't utter a sound. Both gazed at the humans gazing at them.

Most writers treated the gorilla "nuptials" with a light touch, and practically every daily newspaper in this country, and many abroad, carried stories and pictures, which pleased Butler and his staff.

Gaily colored posters introducing "Mr. and Mrs. Gargantua the Great" appeared on billboards and barnsides throughout the country, with the circus title in block letters and a line across the bottom reading "For 60 years The Greatest Show on Earth."

By now the circus press department referred to Toto as M' Toto or Mademoiselle Toto because it claimed she was captured in the French Congo and had spent some time in Paris. Anything to create publicity.

On tour, the gorillas could be seen in a tent near the Big Top with a sign, "Gorilla Land, Home of Gargantua and M' Toto." No matter what the weather, patrons stood in line to buy tickets.

Roland Butler recognized the possibilities for publicity and never missed an opportunity. Circus Christmas cards that year featured Gargantua and M' Toto with heads together surrounded by a wreath of holly with the words, "Mr. and Mrs. Gargantua the Great Wish you a Merry Christmas and a Happy New Year."

A full-color poster showing the gorillas and the slogan, "Buy War Bonds," a popular theme of the times, raised many millions for the war effort.

Wherever he went, reporters asked Roland about the gorillas, inquiring about their health, eating habits, exercises, and daily routine. He produced a copy of feeding instructions which told when, what, and how much of each item the apes would be given in their daily diet.

Some inquired whether they indulged in sex, and if they might have offspring. While the circus had always skirted the subject of sex, Roland had done a job with M' Toto's pictures, painting on ample breasts. Actually, her mammary glands were little larger than Gargantua's — small protrusions hidden by shaggy hair.

"You know," Roland would replay; "it's very likely they'll have babies, just like in the wild. It's a very tender, touching thing. I mean the affection they seem to have for each other. Naturally, bein' the only two gorillas around, they'd be interested in each other.

"Tell you the truth, I haven't had a chance to check on their sex life, but I will, by God! I must ask Dick Kroener and Jose Tomas. They'll give us the straight dope.

"I wouldn't be at all surprised. Who knows? Next year we may have a baby or two, by God! Wouldn't that be a pip?"

With that he'd put on his hat and bow out of the city room, a smile on his face. He was a genius at planting little stories and reaping a rich harvest in publicity. Often such gems appeared in a box on the front page. One was about the peanut.

Well into the season he reported he'd checked with concessions men and they'd given him some interesting news — the performance that year was the most exciting and thrilling in history. Newsmen demanded an explanation. "What was the basis for such a statement? Was it an assumption?"

"Hell, no!" he bellowed. "We never go on assumptions. It's based on the amount of peanuts being eaten. We're sellin' more

Roland Butler designed cards and advertising matter for many circuses, especially after his association with the Ringling show ended. These are some of his best.

peanuts than ever before; we buy 'em by the carload, you know. When acts are dangerous; and nerve tingling, people eat peanuts by the peck.

"I'd say we're averaging at least a ton a day; the jumbo size, of course. Such things tell a lot about business; it's a fact. Concessions men tell me it's a real barometer, you understand?"

One almost had to believe Roland Butler's stories because he told them with such candor and enthusiasm. Like the one about the giraffe with a sore throat. When it first appeared in local papers the wire service picked it up. Butler liked to repeat it, and swore it was true.

"This old giraffe had a neck about six feet long and a chronic sore throat," he would begin. "It took half a bottle of whiskey to bring relief; nothing but the finest Kentucky bourbon. The show carried five cases of the stuff to keep the old boy comfortable and on his feet.

"Once in Texas the sheriff in one of those backwoods counties took the giraffe and his whiskey into custody. We sent out a quick call for the fixer — a lawyer of great renown named Frank Cook. His official title was legal adjuster, and he traveled with the show to settle claims.

"Cook was the smartest man in the business — a damn convincin' talker on any subject. He painted such a dismal picture of the poor, sick giraffe the county dropped the charges, and the sheriff apologized.

"I'm not sure, but I believe we got most of the whiskey back, come to think of it."

Roland could talk himself out of an embarrassing situation as easily and quickly as the circus lawyer. He and Estelle had a dog they called Breeches Boy and sometimes found it necessary to sneak the dog into their hotel.

Once when Roland was taking Breeches Boy for his early morning walk he encountered the hotel's security chief in the hall.

"What about that dog?" the house dick growled, pointing an accusing finger. "We don't allow dogs, you know. No sir!"

"Hadn't you heard?" Butler asked in surprise. "Why don't they tell you what's goin' on around here? You know this place is full of rats. Well, this is the best rat-catcher in America. Management knows he's here to clean the place up. I'm surprised they didn't tell you."

With that he resumed his walk with Breeches Boy.

Through 1940 and most of 1941 the threat of war was commencing to be felt in America. Thousands of young men and women went into military service, many from the circus. Others found jobs in defense plants, trying out the new forty-hour workweek.

The musicians union began making demands that John Ringling North refused to meet, and late in May 1941 Merle Evans and his band were pulled off the show in Philadelphia. A feature that season was an elephant ballet that included special music and costuming.

Anticipating that negotiations might fail, officials had recorded the entire performance on tape. When the band left, it used the tapes. Evans, who had never finished high school, was hired as band director at Hardin Simmons University in Abilene, Texas, where he enjoyed his role as "professor" without benefit of a college degree.

North invited the band leader to go back on the show, but Evans refused.

"I've been a union musician all my life," he reminded the circus president. "If I went back now, I'd never be able to work again."

Another loss occurred near the end of the 1941 tour when eleven elephants were mysteriously poisoned and died on the circus grounds in Charlotte, N.C. A month later, on December 7, America entered World War II.

Tire and gasoline rationing, blackouts, and other restrictions made it difficult for

Forrest Freeland and Butler were friends for years but severed relations. Freeland continued to use this letterhead which Butler designed for the Clyde Beatty-Cole Bros. Circus.

all circuses. There were no new acts or attractions, but the press department carried on, emphasizing gaiety and laughter. The circus pushed the sale of war bonds at every performance, and men and women in uniform were admitted free.

The press department included Butler, Braden, Allen Lester, Bernie Head, Don McCloud, and, of course, Estelle Butler. The radio department was run by Beverly Kelley and Frank L. Morrissey. All worked closely with newspaper and radio sources, and it paid off.

"The circus has arrived," the *New York Times* announced that spring, "suitably heralded with adjectives by Mr. Roland Butler, and in a time when nothing else is normal in the world, it is in its normal manner bigger and better than ever.

"It has been our instructive pleasure for several seasons to study the publicity efforts of the advance agents of Ringling Bros and Barnum & Bailey. These may, to the casual observer, seem to follow an identical pattern year after year; simply a visit to newspaper offices to unload a great string of resounding alliterative polysyllables — accompanied, of course, by passes. Nothing could be farther from the truth.

"The year's publicity must have a Theme. One season, stress will be laid on Alfred Court and his greatest of all wild animal acts, with its attendant — and very real — dangers. Then Norman Bel Geddes will be brought in to streamline the whole circus, and this will be the theme. This year General Press Representative Butler, his ear to the ground and his hand on the pulse of the public as befits a man in his trade, has hit astutely on the theme of Gayety.

"This is shrewd showmanship for wartime, because, as Hollywood itself has discovered without much trouble, people who go to amusements in wartime want to be amused. The circus has always been noisily, although sometimes a little pondorously, gay. This year we may expect a notable outburst of gayety which will verge perhaps on frivolity. So much the better.

"We observed in the interviews this spring with Mr. Butler a new candor, also in keeping with the self-searching times. He is tacitly willing to admit that mistakes have been made in previous circus seasons. Speaking of the clowns, he says, 'We've been using them too little.' This squares nicely with our own observations, made from the vantage point of a boxful of noisy children in the Garden. Let us by all means give the clowns their chance this year of all years.

"There is also an implication of self-criticism in the remark that there will be 'No heavy historical stuff this year.' This indicates, of course, that things may have been a trifle heavy at times in the past."

The North brothers and Concello proposed two possibilities for the circus during the war — operate as a nonprofit organization with government approval and support, or stay in winter quarters.

"Nothing doing," a majority of directors said. "The show must go on."

North's five-year term as president expired in 1942, and the 49ers took over, with Robert E. Ringling as president. The only son of Charles and Edith Ringling, he was more qualified as a Chicago opera singer, which he had been, than a circus executive.

James A. Haley, who had been John Ringling's accountant, was named vice president and assistant to the president. The following year he married Aubrey Ringling, widow of Alf T.'s son, Richard, who owned a third of the show.

CHAPTER FIFTEEN

Newspapers continued to give the circus generous treatment. After all, there wasn't much to cheer about in those dark days, and Roland Butler always brought them a few moments of merriment.

"Here's a man who knows more newspapermen than any other individual in the world," wrote Ted Roper of the *Columbus (Ohio) Dispatch* in 1943.

"He's Roland Butler, the press agent extraordinary, spinner of super-interesting tales, hail fellow well met, and officially in charge of press relations for the Ringling Bros and Barnum & Bailey Circus, coming to Columbus for four performances Monday and Tuesday.

"Along in the spring sometime (until this year when the circus arrives nearly three months later than its usual date) Roland ambles into the *Dispatch* editorial department, toting his familiar brown briefcase. As he walks, he starts greeting his friends and waving. He never misses a first name, in spite of the fact that he hasn't seen the man for a whole year.

"In his briefcase are stories and pictures of 'The Greatest Show in the World.' His job is 'planting' the publicity on receptive desks in the newspapers of the United States."

Roper's description of Butler was accurate and similar to others year after year. When Butler arrived in New York for the opening of the 1944 tour, the *Times* announced it in these words:

"The man with the exploding adjectives is in town. 'Gather around and hear about the most magnificent and exhilarating spectacle ever beheld by mortal eye, unparalleled in amusement annals,' he boomed. He should know. He is Roland Butler, the head press agent of Ringling Bros and Barnum & Bailey Circus.

"This Butler is not a man given to the simple motif. The Butler Thesaurus is one of perennial exhaltation. 'In unraveling its manifold marvels before the eyes of the Big Show's spectators,' he says, 'the gigantic 1944 performance clearly reflects the Ringling genius of its production staff. There are scores of exciting displays, each composed of several individual acts overflowing the arena, the vast hippodrome oval, and taxing to the utmost the vast space of the Garden.' Then Butler wound up:

"'For the young and old, we give you Emmett Kelly in "Panto's Paradise," a funfeast. Our Emmett is the master of the melancholy mood. This truly great Big Top comedian believes that laughter is the byproduct of sorrow, or at any rate of sympathy; he brings crowds to the verge of tears before he makes them laugh.'

"And of course there will be the 'inimitable' display of educated man-killers in Alfred Court's wild animal acts."

Kelly was not among the veteran clowns on the show at one time, nor was he the most inventive and imaginative, but he was popular with the people, and Butler knew it. The Weary Willie character Kelly portrayed was a favorite with everybody.

As Butler had promised the *Times,* there were more clown numbers that season, with Kelly, Lou Jacobs, Harry Ritley, Paul Jung, Felix Adler, Bumps Anthony, Jerry Bangs, Frankie Saluto, Jimmy Armstrong, Paul Jerome, Otto Griebling, Bill Ballentine, Paul Wenzel, and others.

Merle Evans and his band were back, in snappy new uniforms. Robert Ringling, who had a real appreciation for music, called Evans and wanted him to have plenty of brass. He insisted on four French horns and four tubas. Somehow, from somewhere, Ringling acquired four Bayreuth tubas, German-made with French horn mouthpieces. Merle Evans still insists they came from the Metropolitan Opera.

"The only place we could get those tubas was the Metropolitan Opera in New York," according to Merle. "The Metropolitan wanted a horse, so we traded them a white horse for those four tubas."

When Merle decided to get rid of the tubas, it gave Roland Butler an idea, and he used it to advantage.

"The circus is going to get rid of those old tubas in the band at last," he announced to the press, "and replace them with more worthy musical instruments."

Several newspapers took the bait and jumped on the press agent. Some considered his remarks derogatory, and a few actually took umbrage — in a friendly sort of way. One of these was the *Richmond* (Va.) *Times-Dispatch,* which editorially disputed Butler's description of the tuba's sound as "umpah."

"By 'umpah,'" the newspaper said, "Mr. Butler means (and these are his words) 'that diabolical instrument, the old fashioned tuba,' There will be no tubas in the circus band from now on, says he.

"Mr. Butler evidently is a man who has no ear for music. The sound made by the tuba is not 'umpah' as alleged, but 'oompah.' Mark our words, Mr. Butler is going to hear from the customers."

He did, in an avalanche of letters, phone calls, and editorials. Even the *New York Times* came to the defense of the tuba, claiming the instrument represented the minority and its rights must be protected.

"Lovers of the tuba are of the quiet, brooding sort; slow to anger and slow to forgive," it observed. "They are sensitive, and it is safe to say that Mr. Butler has permanently alienated them."

"My God!" Butler exclaimed in astonishment. "I never had any idea the noisy old piece of plumbing had such a following. I never meant to offend anybody, for Christ's sake!"

Merle Evans said he finally disposed of the tubas — "Sold 'em to a fellow in California."

By now America was deeply involved in World War II, fighting in the Atlantic and Pacific, on land and in the air. The Ringling Bros and Barnum & Bailey Circus itself had sent 887 men and women into the armed forces and was forced to operate with few experienced hands.

Coming out of Florida winter quarters, it opened in Madison Square Garden on April 5 and stayed until May 21. Then it moved to Boston, Philadelphia, Waterbury, New Haven, and Bridgeport, Connecticut; Worcester and Fitchburg, Massachusetts; Manchester, Portland, and Providence.

Circus trains were late reaching Harford from Providence on July 5, 1944, and the afternoon performance was canceled. The show drew only a fair crowd that night.

In the middle of the next afternoon, July 6, the most disastrous event in the history of the circus in America occurred when fire broke out in the Big Top. Most of the 6,789 patrons fled in panic, but 168 of them died. Another 682 suffered burns or other injuries, among them 60 circus employees.

Roland Butler was in Springfield, Massachusetts, that day and hurried to Hartford when word reached him. He opened an office there and worked with Herbert DuVal, legal adjuster, for the next several days,

CIRCUS HISTORICAL SOCIETY

BANDWAGON

Vol. 6, No. 6   Nov. Dec. 1962

Wishes You a Merry Christmas AND Happy New Year

Butler was working on this Christmas card when he passed away in 1961. Another artist
finished it and Butler's name was dropped from the lower left hand corner.

energetic, ambitious, and shrewd entrepreneur became at age forty-four the first man ever to have control of "The Greatest Show on Earth."

Butler and his staff were blamed for much adverse publicity after the Hartford fire. It wasn't true, of course, but it made the season a nightmare. Roland considered such allegations an outrage.

All circuses began to feel the pinch, as cities and even counties began adopting or enforcing strict ordinances against them.

"I have had twenty wonderful years with a wonderful firm," Roland Butler said when it was announced at the end of the season that he had retired. "It's about time I laid up and got a little pasture."

He refused to elaborate, but many suspected it wasn't the real story. He was fully aware of the discord and distrust among owners, directors, and officials of the great old circus, and he left quietly.

CHAPTER SIXTEEN

NEWS OF BUTLER'S "retirement" shocked editors, columnists, reporters, and photographers on the nation's newspapers and magazines as much as it surprised the circus world, and it brought comment.

Although his visits were brief and only once a year, he had earned their friendship and trust. They remembered him and were happy to give him space because his copy was always timely and interesting.

His feature stories and pictures were an editor's delight, for they were clear and professionally prepared. He always called on editorialists in a happy and receptive mood and thus was able to gain more publicity in more newspapers than any other press agent of his time, both in news and editorial columns.

Outside of newspaper and magazine connections, the Butlers had few close personal friends. As one long-time admirer summed it up:

"Although they may not have been numerous, I think he had as many friends as he wanted."

Word that Butler had retired brought comment from newspapers all across the country.

The *Sarasota Herald-Tribune,* published in the circus' hometown, commented:

"As much a part of 'The Greatest Show on Earth' as the elephants, Butler's adjectives and superlatives have festooned every newspaper in the United States.

"From Maine to California and from Florida to Washington, Butler is known in every city room of every major paper in the country. Since 1929 he has headed the staff of press agents, photographers and contracting press agents exploiting elephants, pretty girls, aerial stars and workingmen alike."

The *Memphis Commercial Appeal* editorialized:

"Long before billboards told of its coming, and a shrieking calliope announced its arrival, American newspapers knew the circus was headed for town, especially if it happened to be the Ringling Brothers show.

"Roland Butler's appearance in any editorial room was all any editor and his staff needed to tell them that the circus wasn't far behind.

"General press representative of Ringling Brothers for two decades, Roland Butler was the circus's official herald, and in his field they didn't come better. He usually got what he wanted, and he never asked or expected the impossible.

"The news of his retirement has an ominous hint about it — that perhaps the circus he so long represented won't be taking to the road next spring. It has had hard luck from circumstances beyond its control, and perhaps a decision to stay off the road has been necessary. We hope not, yet can't imagine anything else causing Roland Butler to give up something he loved so much. He was part of the circus, and the circus was part of him.

"Whatever the real motive, American newspaper offices are going to miss him."

David E. Smiley of the *Tampa Times* called him "an astute judge of popular trends and an able showman."

"Roland Butler is an ambassador of high type," wrote Lew Heck of the *Cincinnati Times Star*. "He visits editors with the grace of a king's representative."

George Brinton Beal of the *Boston Sunday Post* observed:

"Roland Butler is blessed with a rainbow eye and a joyous vocabulary. There is no limit in the enchantment of his word pictures."

Alan Morley of the *Vancouver Sun* wrote:

"Roland Butler, famous publicist, loves the profession he is in, respects it, and in turn lends it some of his own class."

C. E. Broughton of the *Sheboygan Press* called him "frank, congenial and convincing."

"I offered to make Roland Butler a guest columnist for a day if he would write about himself," wrote Paul Light of the *St. Paul Pioneer Press*. "He established a record by refusing. He'd rather publicize the big show he is paid to represent."

Conrad Frederick Smith of the *Charlotte Observer* referred to him as "genial Roland Butler, America's No. 1 publicity man."

"The circus arrives Saturday for a two-day stand at Cumminsville and Roland Butler's release is something new and different," wrote E. B. Radcliffe of the *Cincinnati Enquirer*, and added:

"As informative as a restaurant bill of fare where dishes are listed in English, as accurate as a time table and almost as coldly factual as an itemized monthly statement on a department store charge account, the Butler 'Circus News Program,' with its eight subdivisions of information is a serviceable item of condensation of the 'who, what, when, where, why and how' of the big show."

Harvey Hough of the *Springfield* (Ohio) *News* wrote:

"Roland Butler has something that most press agents usually lack, and that is a genuine knowledge of the 'science of the circus' and an interest in passing that on to the uninitiated."

When Butler called on Frank Francis of the *Ogden* (Utah) *Standard-Examiner*, the columnist wrote:

"Though he had not seen me in seven years, his memory is so keen he called me by name without an introduction. He is a genial fellow and has many friends who welcome him on his annual circus tour of the United States."

The *New York Times* called him "press agent extraordinary," and the *Beaumont* (Texas) *Journal* said he was a "noted public relations expert."

"Roland Butler, the most widely known publicist today, courts only legitimate publicity," said the *Juneau* (Alaska) *Evening Empire*. "That is why he has made such a success of his far-flung job."

The *Philadelphia Evening Bulletin* called him, "Minister plenipotentiary from the Kingdom of Publicity," and the *Davenport* (Iowa) *Democrat and Leader* said Butler "has grown to be an American institution."

"Roland Butler has arrived in Bridgeport," observed Edward J. Shugrue of the *Bridgeport Sunday Post*. "So has an abundance of colorful copy bearing the unmistakable imprint of his master hand.

"The world-renowned publicity man always loves to visit the city that P. T. Barnum made famous.

"Yesterday I went on an inspection tour with Roland. He wanted to discover if it were true that the bronze base of the Barnum monument is 'hollow.' It is.

" 'But his head wasn't,' the publicity man expounded. Neither is Squire Butler's."

Arthur M. Concello, triple-somersault star, bought the Russell Bros. Circus from Claude Webb. It was based in California, and Butler joined his old friend there as di-

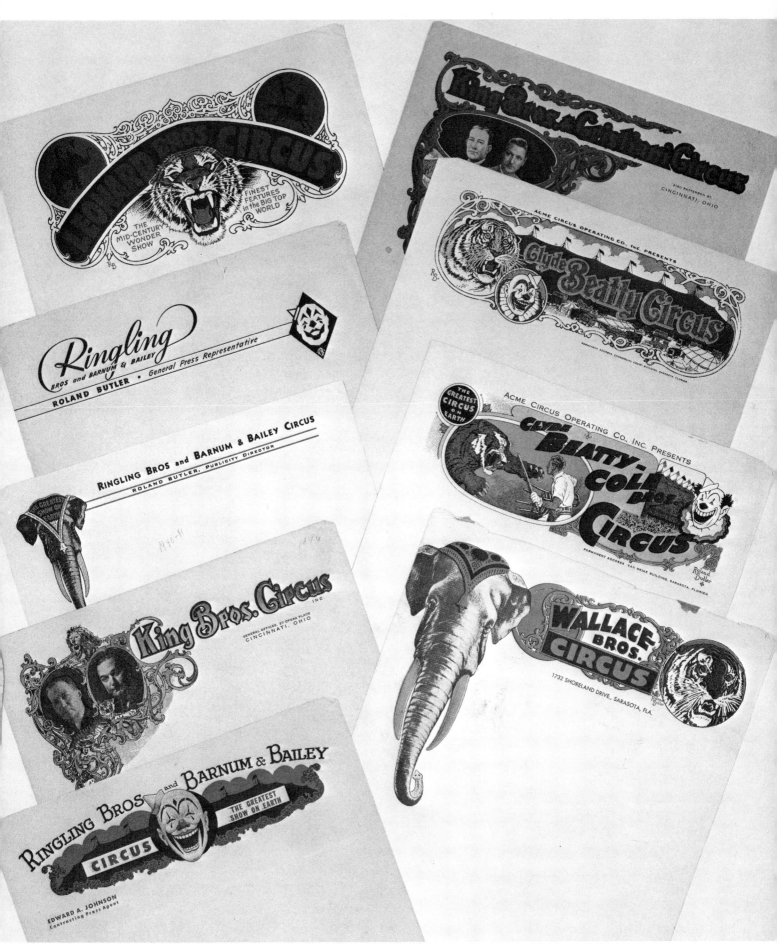

Butler designed letterheads and other literature for many circuses. He was proud of his art work
and usually put his name or initials on his productions such as these.

rector of press and publicity. William B. Antes was director of radio, working with Butler.

The Russell Bros. Great Pan Pacific Circus toured California, Oregon, and Washington using the slogan, "The highest class traveling amusement organization on earth."

Butler received only a modest salary but was happy to be working as a circus press agent again, especially with Concello. Estelle said later she was paid $35 a week to drive Roland on his rounds and saved every dime of it. When asked about this, Concello would say only that "press agents didn't make much money."

World War II was still on, and Concello's Russell Bros. Circus found it rough going. It went off the road at the end of the 1945 tour.

The Butlers returned to Florida and bought a comfortable old house on a quarter of a block at 706 Fourth Street in Palmetto, a quiet farming community across the Manatee River from Bradenton and a dozen miles north of Sarasota.

The house, shaded by moss-draped oaks, faced a street which had been paved with red bricks many years before. Built of wood, it was painted white with green trim and with green shutters on the windows.

It had a main floor and an attic, and there was a carport, utility room, and small cottage in the rear. They rented the cottage for a season or two to winter visitors.

It was close enough to Sarasota so they could keep in touch with circus friends there, yet it provided privacy when they wished. It was a nice spot to retire in, but Roland had no intention of that.

Idleness galled him, and he joined William W. Perry, former *Sarasota Tribune* newsman, state legislator, and politician, to form The Florida Service, Inc., dealing in public relations, creative advertising, and offset printing. The venture soon ended.

Butler set up an office in the guest cottage, where he turned out letterheads, pro-grams, posters, and other printed matter, mostly for circuses. The place soon was filled with his large collection of circusiana, including lithographs, route books, heralds, and opposition "rat" bills.

He had collected everything from 100-year-old posters and lithographs to letter openers, postcards, and newspaper clippings. There were stacks of photographs in cardboard boxes, framed lithos piled in corners, and other circus matter scattered about. The utility room, just off the back steps of the house, was full and so was the attic.

Sunburst wheels from old parade wagons marked the entrance off the street; dozens of others were propped about the grounds. They were of assorted sizes and in various stages of disrepair.

For twenty-five years the circus had been the Butlers' lives, and they missed it. At sixty and still in vigorous health, it galled him to be virtually "retired" from the challenges and friendships he'd known for so many years — when he might have been calling on friends coast to coast, talking with them about the circus, and entertaining them with stories.

He passed the time pawing through stacks of circus matter and compiling a list of what he had. He made a little money designing Christmas cards, letterheads, and other printed matter.

Floyd King recalled that when he operated the King Bros. Circus, Roland drew all his advertisements and designed his Christmas cards.

"He was the finest fellow I ever did business with," King said. "He always believed in fair dealing.

"One fall while the circus was near Bradenton, I went over to Roland's house and asked him what I owed him for work he'd done for King Bros. Circus. He said $156. I reached in my hip pocket and pulled out the exact amount, as I had previously had a bill from him for the work.

"He said he did not plan on seeing my

One of Butler's specialties was Christmas cards. Here are two examples for one of his favorite circuses, Clyde Beatty-Cole Bros.

circus in Bradenton, but that afternoon he and his wife came over. Art Concello and quite a number of retired owners and managers were there. They never saw the performance, but they were under a shade awning of the ticket wagon, and many a story was told there."

Roland kept abreast of circus doings through friends on and off the lot. When John Ringling North returned as executive vice president in 1947, with Haley as president, Butler had hopes of going back, too.

Concello returned as general manager. Kelley was publicity director and would have been glad to have Butler back, but there was room for only one more in he press department.

"Frank Braden will die if he doesn't get an invitation to come back," John Ringling North told Kelley.

So Braden got the job, and Butler had to wait another year. He passed it in nervous anxiety, assembling some of his memorabilia and selling it. The circus was his life, and he couldn't survive without a part of it.

"Roland's stellar performance, when he really had something to work on," his friend Bev Kelley recalled, "nowhere is better illustrated than in his publicity campaign (including designs for posters) for the Ubangis and the giraffe-neck women from Burma, and in the 1938 season for Gargantua's debut with Frank ("Bring 'Em Back Alive") Buck and the handsomest spec (Nepal) I can recall through many seasons.

"I think these milestones rank with those from the time of Tom Thumb and Jumbo, and I don't doubt that had our friend been operating in those days he would have improved upon them.

"Another of the Butler accomplishments remain in use to this day and is almost the only redeeming feature of some pretty attractive Ringling Bros and Barnum & Bailey Circus newspaper advertisements I've seen. This is Roland's wonderful fat circus titles that jump right off the page.

"When I had to make new advertisements during the time he was off the show, I never altered his titles; they could not be improved."

Butler liked to do his friends of the newspaper profession a favor, and he could find a feature with a circus flavor any time he wished. Once when a wire service reporter needed a story, Roland escorted him to Joe Dan Miller, a general handyman the press agent claimed had been "with it" for sixty-five or seventy of his eighty years on earth.

Miller had worked in many departments of the show and knew everyone connected with it, the walls of his Sarasota home were covered with postcards and photographs from all over America. But he was reluctant to talk to a strange reporter, and Butler asked and answered most of the questions while Miller nodded or shook his head.

Back in the press car, Roland completed the story, thusly:

"They'll never put old Joe Dan in a pauper's grave, by God! He's got it all figured out, like most circus folks — they make funeral plans ahead.

"The undertaker in Joe Dan's hometown of Jackson, Tennessee, is Ewing Griffin, who's the sheriff, too. Every time the show plays Memphis, Joe Dan takes off for Jackson to inspect his shroud and casket. It's a fact.

"His burial outfit, as I understand, is hanging in a cedar bag on the wall, right by the casket he picked out. Last time Joe Dan was there, he climbed into the casket to try it out and forgot to take off his muddy boots. They had to take out the lining and send it to the cleaners. That's a goddamn fact.

"I doubt like hell if Joe Dan'll ever go back there, alive!"

The story appeared in newspapers across the land, but whether the casket and shroud ever existed is questionable. As Roland Butler would say, "Who the hell knew the difference?"

When Joe Dan passed on, funeral services were held in Sarasota, and the remains were cremated in nearby St. Petersburg. Among circus friends at the funeral was Jim Haley, executive vice president at the time.

To this day some suggest Butler's story of the casket and shroud was fabricated to give a reporter a story and add to the legend of Joe Dan Miller.

CHAPTER SEVENTEEN

ROLAND BUTLER denied that John Ringling fired him late in 1926 after Charles passed away, but he insisted he was fired in 1944.

"I resigned from the Ringling Show in 1926 after Mr. Charlie passed away," he said, "but I was fired in '44 and I mean fired, by God! I want to get that straight in the press once and for all.

"I consider it no dishonor to have been fired by previous management, but I've never been fired by any professional showman, including the Ringlings, and that's a cold, hard fact. Put that down in black and white. They kicked Johnny North out in 1942, but he came back in '47 as president, which was a damn smart move.

"Mr. North will give the show professional and experienced management. He's a top showman; smart as his old Uncle John, by God! This 1948 edition looks like a terrific production. There'll be a lot more for the kids and, after all, ain't the circus for kids? There'll be a lot more great new European acts new to America, too. I want to emphasize that fact."

Butler was back with the show now, long before the 1954 upheaval that sent him home for good.

"We'll have the press department back the way it was when Mr. North was in command," he added. "We'll have Frank Braden, Eddie Johnson, Bill Fields, and Gardner Wilson — all professionals with years of experience.

"I'll probably have the old title of general press representative or publicity direc-
tor; it won't make any difference. I'm not a detailist son of a bitch and never was. I don't give a damn about a title. I'm just a circus press agent, that's all.

"I'll lay out itineraries, handle newspaper copy, and divide up towns with others. Bill Antes and Murray Burt will handle radio. Stelle will drive me, of course; nearly all our travelin' will be by car.

"There'll be no letdown in our copy; hell no!" he added in thunderous tones, an obvious slap at his predecessors. "We won't tolerate silly, hogwash copy; never would when I was around. We'll stick to strong language, with plenty of punch and conviction, you bet.

"We'll try to keep our copy crisp and colorful for the thousand or more newspapers we deal with around the country. We put out about twenty-five different releases during the month the show's playing New York. That's a hell of a lot, don't you agree?

"Incidentally, New York's a nightmare for me. Soon as I check into the Piccadilly Hotel people start callin' — they know the circus is comin', and they want passes, ads, souvenirs; everything.

"When I register I don't even tell them I'm with the show, but somehow word leaks out, and they pester me night and day. It's fiendish! I'd much rather be in Chicago or Memphis or Houston; Minneapolis or Frisco — any one of a hundred places outside New York."

During war years the popular route book

came out in paperback but now returned to hard-cover format, fatter than ever with eighty-two pages filled with facts and figures about the annual tour.

A compact volume four by six inches, it contained the names of all circus personnel, officers, and directors; routes, with mileage between cities; program and routes of previous years since 1919. It was a treasury of information prized by circus people and collectors.

The book also contained stories about star performers and circus operations. This time there was a feature on the new portable grandstand with folding upholstered seats invented by Art Concello.

"Where it once took 250 men four hours to do the job," the route book said, "this year it has been completed in an hour by four superintendents and ten co-workers.

"The seats of the portable steel grandstand are literally built around the dual-wheeled trucks used to transport it, folding flat and into the sides and tops. Steel safety stairways are part of the mobile package."

Writing about one of his favorite cities, Butler let himself go with this account of the circus in San Francisco's Cow Palace:

"The Ringling Bros and Barnum & Bailey Circus established a profitable precedent during its tented tour this year when it switched from canvas to concrete and gave seven capacity performances inside San Francisco's mammoth Cow Palace. Never before in all its glorious history had the Big Show exhibited in a building anywhere outside New York and Boston.

"Belying its unglamorous title, the Cow Palace, a superb indoor ampitheatre building, planned in genius and vision, without a pillar, post or overhanging balcony to obstruct the view from a single one of the 13,294 seats occupied during the circus' stay, proved to be the long lost lodestone of California's great Bay City. . . .

"From a standpoint of daily remuneration, the Cow Palace engagement was the most profitable ever played during any circus tour in the history of the world."

Closing number in that 1949 season was entitled "The Glorious Fourth" and was billed as a "spectacular, American, magnificent finale, vibrant with pageantry, color, beauty, song, and patriotic thrills," featuring "The Glorious Fourth with its proud, rousing, heart-clutching tableau, 'The land of the free and home of the brave,' dedicated to all the free peoples of the earth and to our President."

The route book and press releases chronicled that Cecil B. De Mille, motion picture producer and director, joined that summer to get the "feel" of the circus and plan his movie, "The Greatest Show on Earth."

The circus had all its old standbys, including the Guistino Loyals, Unus, Francis Brunn, Hugo Schmitt and his elephants, La Norma, the Flying Concellos, and the Alzanas, along with Merle Evans and his band as well as some new attractions.

On the last day of the season, November 25 at Miami, Gargantua the Great was found dead in his cage. The word was flashed on Associated Press wires, treatment reserved for news of great import.

"He was a real trouper to the end," Roland Butler said. "We billed him above the humans; he was a bigger drawing card than Elvis Presley, Bing Crosby, Bob Hope, or any other star of stage, screen, and radio. There'll never be another attraction like Gargantua, by God!"

The tour had covered 18,948 miles over 32 different railroads, and the 415 performances drew 3,473,000 patrons. After a few days in winter quarters, most acts and attractions went by ship and plane to Cuba for a thirty-two-day engagement in Havana's Sports Palace.

In his book, *Center Ring*, author Robert Lewis Taylor described Butler's predicament leading to the Havana opening two weeks after Gargantua's death.

"On every available wall there," Taylor

wrote, "Butler had posters on which the word 'Gargantua' overshadowed all the other copy. He was obliged to pick up a paint can and brush and run all over town painting in a gigantic 'Mrs.' before the magic word.

"The circus had lately bought a female gorilla named Toto — by chance from an American woman living in Havana — with the idea of promoting a union.

" 'This Toto's a Havana girl,' said Butler, explaining to North his sprint with the paint can. 'It gives the gorilla stuff a local angle, see?' "

The Havana stand extended through the holidays and into 1950. In the route book for that year Butler described the show's visit with his usual enthusiasm.

"Playing through the holidays to capacity crowds and turning thousands away during the final week, the circus closed in a blaze of glory Sunday night, January 8, 1950, and chalked up a smashing success. . . .

"Havana went wild over the performances and gave The Greatest Show on Earth the warmest reception it ever accorded a visiting amusement organization. . . .

"Still circus hungry at the close of the run, the Cuban capital's press and public implored the Big Show to hurry back and make the Havana engagement an annual event."

The circus played postseason dates in Havana in 1955 and 1956.

Gargantua's death was a staggering blow. Someone in the press department suggested they wear armbands of black during a brief period of mourning.

"That's one hell of an idea," Butler agreed. "Wish I'd thought of it."

Circus officials hoped to exhibit the body, according to Dr. S. Dillon Ripley, then curator of vertebrate zoology in the Peabody Museum at Yale University and now secretary of the Smithsonian Institution in Washington, who wrote:

"John Ringling North, head of the circus, offered Gargantua to the Peabody Museum at Yale when he died, on condition that we have the skin mounted and return it to the circus as a traveling attraction. Yale would, of course, have gotten little but a lot of extra work out of this.

"The hacked-up carcass was sent on to us, and we preserved the skeleton, which is on exhibition here. We never saw the original body."

Gargantua's body was flown by National Airlines from Miami to Johns Hopkins Hospital in Baltimore, where an autopsy was performed and studies made of the gorilla's skin cancer and other ailments.

According to Dr. Ripley, Gargantua was not the largest nor the oldest gorilla in captivity. He was five feet seven and one-half inches tall and weighed 312 pounds, the scientist reported.

A gorilla named Massa, also raised by Mrs. Gertrude Lintz, is reported to weigh about 450 pounds. He celebrated his fifty-first birthday at Christmastime in 1981 at the Philadelphia Zoo, where he has been since 1935. The zoo claims Massa is the oldest gorilla in captivity.

In any event, publicity generated by Roland Butler and his staff made Gargantua the Great the best-known circus animal since Barnum's elephant Jumbo, and the most famous gorilla in history.

With the 1949 season that extended through the holidays and into January over at last, Butler went to work answering the flow of letters that increased when the circus was off the road. There were inquiries into every phase of the operation, and often requests for photographs.

A woman in Marblehead, Massachusetts, said she was writing a book and wanted to know if a mule could sit, and if so for how long. She wrote that the Museum of Comparative Zoology at Harvard had no authoritative information and had referred her to the circus. She stated she had a deadline to meet and needed a swift reply.

"We thank you for your letter of January

Blue and yellow flags were added to the Butler Christmas card and this is the finished product. The card was used for some time after the press agent's death.

"7," Butler replied. "Of course a mule can sit upon its buttocks, or 'bottom' as you term it in your letter. I remember that my grandmother used to call it 'bottom' when I was a boy in New England.

"Your illustration is entirely correct, showing the two forelegs upright while the mule sits in the same manner as a dog does. Some mules are trained to sit down; others sit down of their own initiatives. The temperament and behavior of all mules is not identical.

"The length of time they sit varies, the same as it does with other sitting creatures. Obviously, trainers have little or no difficulty teaching mules to sit down, but the animals can be stubborn, and often it requires patience.

"We trust that the above information is that which you desire in order to meet the deadline on your forthcoming book; and also to place in the files of the Harvard University Museum of Comparative Zoology."

Most facts sought by letter writers came from Butler's own store of knowledge or observation, but if he was in doubt he'd hurry to one of the dens or cages and inquire of a keeper.

"The folks who give us giant-size headaches are real circus fans," he said, shuffling the mail. "We get letters from all over the United States and Canada; some even from foreign countries, for Christ's sake!

"You ever see some of the model circuses they build? They're not circus buffs or historians but real technicians — skillful and patient as hell. They roam all over the backyard, measuring everything from a wagon wheel to an elephant's toenail. God knows how many pictures they take.

"They'll use thread, wooden matches, glue, toothpicks, chewing gum, nylon, canvas, cardboard, and paint of all colors. Everything's to scale and realistic as hell, with the flag up on the cookhouse and clothes dryin' in the backyard. Some paint faces on clowns so accurate they're recognizable.

"They build to scale — quarter inch, half inch, one inch — you name it. They make parade wagons, railroad cars; a lot of animals and props; even patrons in the seats!

"Damn fine productions; authentic all the way. Some models are energized so they actually light up and operate; performers move, and the calliope puffs smoke along with music.

"Every town has an assortment of circus buffs who crowd around to greet friends when the show gets in. Some bring all sorts of things to eat — hams, turkeys, baked chickens, cakes, pies, preserves — everything. They invite performers to dinner in their homes; a real show of fellowship.

"They're real folks who love the circus and its people, and we love them, by God!"

One of Butler's favorite newspapers was the *New York Times*, and each spring he came up with something new. He felt that generous space in the *Times* augured well for the season.

Columnists especially welcomed him and often wrote about the canny press agent. He often denied he was worth a story, but he seemed to relish them, and he saved every mention of himself as well as of the circus.

"It developed that Mr. Butler has a most wonderful regard for clowns," wrote Irving Spiegel of the *Times* one spring:

> When tenting days are gone and nevermore
> He smells the sawdust and sees the laughing eyes
> I somehow think that on a daisied floor
> He'll turn a somersault in Paradise
> To give some angel-child a glad surprise
> Who never saw a circus clown before.

" 'The poet was a Scot by the name of John Ferguson,' said Mr. Butler. And then, on his corniest note, Mr. Butler left, completely exhausted."

Of course. Like every good actor, every Butler appearance was a complete performance, whether his audience was one or ten or more. He liked to entertain, especially members of the press. It brought him exquisite pleasure to see people laugh.

Later, when asked the source of the poem that appeared in Mr. Spiegel's column in the *Times*, Butler smiled and gave one of his characteristic replies:

"I read it in a book somewhere, or maybe on a placard or some other circus literature. What th' hell do I know about poetry? You know I've got a reputation for bein' highly uncouth."

Butler's energy and enthusiasm kept him alert for anything that would keep the circus in the public eye, even when it was in winter quarters. Once during a rare visit to the Charles Ringling home he saw the late Mr. Ringling's mustache cup or shaving mug, an ornate thing with the name inscribed. An idea was born on the spot.

Borrowing the antique, Roland called on George Blood, his friend in the cookhouse, to provide him with four coffee mugs of similar size and shape.

Using paint, gold leaf, and imagination,

Butler converted the mugs to mustache cups of ornate design, complete with saucers. He lettered on the names of Al, Alf T., Otto, and John to match that of Charles — each bold enough to be seen from several feet away.

Behind the display of five shaving mugs he placed a picture of the five brothers and had the collection photographed in color and in black and white.

The picture appeared in a magazine of nationwide circulation a few days before the circus was to begin its tour. The caption called it "The original mustache cups of the famous Ringling brothers, America's premier circus men."

Within days after the magazine came out, an antique dealer from New York showed up at Butler's office and announced he had a buyer for the Ringling mustache cups.

"Not a chance!" Butler roared. "Abso-lutely nothing doing, by God. They're not for sale at any price. The Ringling family would never think of such a thing. Christ, no!"

The dealer explained he had come all the way from New York and was prepared to pay a substantial price. He said he knew the value of such things and asked if he might see them.

"The answer is no!" Butler answered. "Absolutely not. You must not appreciate the finer things of life — little personal items like this. These priceless pieces of porcelain are not on display, and I can tell you they'll never be for sale."

The dealer departed, much to Roland's relief. By this time the mug belonging to the Charles Ringling family had been returned to the big house on the bay, and the others were back in the cookhouse doing duty as coffee mugs.

CHAPTER EIGHTEEN

THE CIRCUS never emphasized the sex angle, and its press agents always played it down, often emphasizing the Ringlings' prohibition against men and women socializing on or off the lot. They were even forbade to meet "accidentally" in cities the circus played.

There was the "virgin car," where sixty-six ballet girls lived; strictly off limits to all males. It was an intriguing subject for reporters, who often inquired what went on there. Roland had a ready answer.

"I can tell you — not a goddamn thing!" he'd shout. "Nobody has time to screw around when the show's on tour. If there's any matin' to be done, it must wait 'til fall when we hit winter quarters.

"Oh, there might be some rare instances, because we're all human beings, for Christ sake! But there's absolutely no privacy unless you have a stateroom, and there's no time when you're doin' two or three shows a day and jumpin' from town to town.

"Once they caught a fellow banging a town girl in a sideshow tent and fined him ten dollars for indecent exposure!

"Anyway, the virgin car is off limits; these broads are well chaperoned, every night. If management caught a man in there, he'd probably be de-balled on the spot; at least kicked off the show."

Roland often used this approach to back the circus's claim that it was a clean operation and did not tolerate tramps of either sex. He'd reel off names of many in personnel who'd been happily married for years. Others were wed on tour or in the off-season, forming unions that have endured to this day. All girls on the show were chaperoned and guarded; rules against fraternizing were rigidly enforced, a fact Butler frequently emphasized.

Circus folk often communicate in vivid and raunchy language, using words towners might regard as vulgar. These must be spoken with a yell or shout to be heard above the noise and confusion of setting up and tearing down.

Butler was gifted in this manner and probably contributed some expressions to a vocabulary of 250 words or more that were gibberish to outsiders. Merle Evans contributed the word "aba-daba," meaning dessert served in the cookhouse.

Butler knew how to wheedle what he needed from others on the show. One day he asked Herbert DuVal, the fixer, to write a piece for the route book detailing some of his experiences with towners trying to fleece the circus.

DuVal's first effort didn't meet with Butler's approval, and the press agent asked him to try again. The second offering was still sprinkled with legalisms and unclear to the average reader.

"Mister DuVal," Butler said sternly on the phone, "this is Roland Butler speakin'. Say, that last thing you sent me for the route book ain't like you. Heat it up; write like you talk. Yeah, to a jury. Give 'em the works, by God! You understand?

"Yeah; tell some of your experiences

with crooked b------- tryin' to f--- us out of everything they can. Give us the real stuff.

"That's it," he conceded after a long pause. "Now you got the idea. Let the words flow like s--t through a goose!"

Two visitors in the press car overheard Roland's conversation and realized he was in a mellow mood. They also knew Roland Butler was far ahead of his time in using obscenities and vulgarisms to command attention. This was an opportunity to encourage him.

They discussed topics of the day, one of his favorites being Father Coughlin, who operated out of a radio station in Michigan. Asked if he'd ever seen Father Coughlin's Shrine of the Little Flower, Butler chuckled and said:

"Hell, yes! Several times, over on that hill."

Like troupers everywhere in every year, Butler went out each spring with bouyant confidence and saw each tour as an unparalleled success. Here is an example from his route book:

"During 1951, when prophets of doom at every turn in the amusement world wailed that road-show business is dead forever, the Ringling Bros and Barnum & Bailey organization made a phenomenally successful 17,000-mile coast-to-coast tour of the nation, exhibited in 121 cities in 36 different states, made millions happy and recorded another glorious circus season on the dial of time.

"Its amicable confraternity, circus-goers of both sexes and all shapes and sizes, from toddlers to venerables, enthusiastically acclaimed this year's fast-moving performance which, from a standpoint of audience appeal, surpassed those of any preceding season in all Big Top history. This fact was acknowledged by reviewers throughout the land.

"While some of the writers criticized the general trend toward modernization of the circus, they had to admit that The Greatest Show on Earth is still the most circusy

thing extant and that its trend is in line with that of everything else worthwhile in the Onward March of Progression. And other scribes referred to the Ringling Bros and Barnum & Bailey colossus as THE circus, and commented on it now being alone in the great field it has always dominated."

His account of the tour was crammed with statistics, perhaps for something better to write without repetition, yet this gourmet with words made it nourishing fare for readers everywhere. It began:

"After 18,907 miles of going places, The Greatest Show on Earth has completed its spectacular 1953 coast-to-coast tour and another truly great season has been recorded in the pages of history.

"Like the Arabs who fold their tents and steal away into the night, the Ringling Bros and Barnum & Bailey people wrapped up their city of canvas after the final performance and during the wee hours entrained for the circus' Sarasota, Florida, winter home.

"But one difference between them and the Arabs is that the circus folks have so much more canvas to fold — to wit, 74,000 yards of it in the 39 tents that house the Big Show.

"That's only one of the many heavy statistics which the world's largest circus racked up this year — statistics which weren't apparent to its three million spectators.

"This year's circus season stretched across 219 days, almost two-thirds of a year. In that time the show traveled more than three-quarters of the distance around the earth on its own three long railroad trains — 69 silver-enameled, eighty-foot flat, stock, elephant and sleeping cars which rode the lines of 37 railroad systems.

"The longest run between engagements was the 718-mile safari from Portland, Oregon, to San Franciso; the shortest an 8-mile move from Windsor, Ontario, to Detroit.

"During its 34-week marathon beginning

April first in New York's Madison Square Garden and ending November 22 in Miami, the circus gave 426 performances in 129 cities in 35 states, the District of Columbia and two Canadian provinces.

"If this data suggests tiresome trouping, consider the 1,289 circus people whose lives are coupled with these statistics. Right now they feel the weight of the earth itself, although they love every ounce of the burden.

"The 1,289 personnel represent 35 nationalities and 1,289 appetites. To feed them, the circus chefs prepared something like 3,500 meals a day throughout the season.

"The show's animals, a thousand of them, also presented a big order in the daily diet department. The vegetarians among them did away with 2,252 tons of hay during the tour and 207,000 pounds of horse meat was devoured by the carnivora.

"In terms of real estate, the circus was a big time operator. It covered between 12 and 13 acres at every stop.

"It also showed a lot of power in the electrical department. It operated 15 Diesel plants to generate its own electricity and laid 24,700 feet of cable to carry the current.

"Seventy-two miles of rope were used in the mammoth circus set-up. This cordage, if reduced to a single strand, would more than encirle the globe. The Jacksonville, Florida, Times-Union printed this fact and punned: 'Though the circus always comes to the end of its season, the nation should be thankful that it never comes to the end of its rope.'"

Although no one suspected or knew it at the time, this was to be Roland Butler's last full season with the show. He concluded the account with these lines:

"While the wizards of production and its panel of mechanical experts are burning the midnight oil to master and perfect still greater and more startling innovations in years to come, the Big Show's loyal troupers may well point with pride to their association with the world-renowned Ringling Bros and Barnum & Bailey Circus in 1953, when it reached the highest standard of excellence ever attained by The Greatest Show on Earth."

The program that season extolled several new features, including educated baby elephants — no pygmies this time!

One clown number was billed as "Futile fisticuffs for the championship of clown alley between Puncho Griebling and Slugger Freeman," which wasn't up to Butler's usual promotions. For him the season's most disagreeable chore was publicizing a thin, blond child prodigy named Mister Mistin, Jr., who played the xylophone.

"Imagine!" the veteran press agent growled sotto voce to friends in the press. "Promotin' a kid that's hardly dry behind the ears, for Christ's sake! Of course, he's terrific, but I says to Art [Concello], 'Next thing you know we'll be havin' diaper races around the hippodrome.' It's a helluva situation; makes you wonder what the hell's goin' on."

No matter his feeling, Butler put aside objections and wrote copy extolling virtues of the tiny boy performer, thusly:

"Prodigiously proclaimed phenomenon, John Ringling North's latest and greatest importation; the tiny musical prodigy who has astounded millions in Europe, Asia and Africa; Mister Mistin, Jr., the child wonder of the world."

Mercifully, Roland admitted later, Mister Mistin, Jr. and his xylophone trouped with the Ringlings only one season.

That year's tour was one of the longest and turned out to be quite profitable. The show spent more time in Canada than ever before or since, going to Quebec City from Lewiston, Maine, then Trois Riviers, Cornwall, Montreal, Kingston, Belleville, Guelph, Oshawa, Hamilton, St. Catherines, Brantford, London, and Windsor before returning to the United States at Detroit.

The 1954 tour was one of change and

challenge. Before Trevor Bale displayed his "amazingly accomplished animals" in the center ring there had been changes in stockholders and management.

John Ringling North became president and chairman of the board and Henry Ringling North vice president and assistant to the president.

Irene Ringling Bon Seigneur and James C. Ringling were named vice presidents; George D. Woods, secretary and treasurer; Frank F. McClosky, John F. Reddy, Jr., and Hester Ringling Sanford, assistant secretaries; Edward F. Kelly, assistant vice president; and Noyelles D. Burkhart, assistant treasurer.

Directors included the North brothers, Woods, Mrs. Bon Seigneur, Mrs. Sanford, Theodore D. Buhl, and William P. Dunn. Buhl replaced Herbert DuVal on the board, and Noyelles D. Burkhart replaced DuVal as legal adjuster.

Concello squabbled with his friend, John North, and departed. McClosky became general manager, and Willis E. Lawson was promoted to manager, with Walter Kernan assistant manager.

McClosky, Lawson, and Kernan were experienced circus men, but some of the others were new to the business.

Butler began the season as publicity director, others on the staff being Frank Braden, Allen Lester, Eddie Johnson, William Fields, and, of course, Estelle Butler. Director of radio and television was Norman Carroll, with Charles Schuyler as his assistant.

Stunning news came in June when it was announced that Roland Butler had "retired." His successor was identified as Edward Knoblaugh, a name unkown in circusdom. It also was announced that F. Beverly Kelley had returned as radio and television director.

Butler had accepted his "retirement" announcement in 1944 in good grace, but now he let friends know he didn't leave by choice.

"I have been fired!" he said with finality and some bitterness when he and Estelle arrived at home in Palmetto. "It happened in Elmira, New York, on Sat'day, the 19th of June, by God!

"I was fired, and you can put that down. That's all there was to it. 'Retired.' Horse s--t! You know I'd never planned to quit right in the middle of the season, for Christ's sake! I'm tellin' you exactly what happened. I was fired! Jim to Mollie.

"I'll tell you how it happened: Management brought in some 'friends' [and he emphasized the word] from Buddy North's Navy and CIA days and gave 'em jobs. There'll be more changes, I suppose. Frank Braden's stayin' on as agent for now, but we Butlers were fired. I want that understood by the press. The minute we found out, Stelle and I packed up and got the hell out of Elmira."

It was a shattering experience for both; no advance notice, not even a hint. The circus Butler had known and loved and worked so hard to publicize most favorably for a quarter of a century had somehow cast them aside and moved on.

All the hardships and loneliness of travel; the years of tensions, turmoil, and tragedies they had endured; the happy times and sad times, all wrapped up in a single announcement — retired; a cold, hard statement he swore was not true.

"Retired?" he shouted, incredibly, as if the word caused nausea. "Hell no — fired! I want my friends in the press to know; they'll understand."

Three days had passed, and they were home again; the shock and disappointment had turned to resentment and rancor. They couldn't blame age or ill health. He was sixty-seven years old, and she was fifty-nine, both as healthy and active as they'd always been. Many on the show, they knew, were older than they.

Now they realized they were victims of the winds of change and whims of man, that friendship was worth more in the human marketplace than capability and experience.

A friend suggested, as had been done several times before, that now was the time to write a book about his life, but Butler scoffed at the idea.

"I'm not colorful or newsworthy," he said. "You'd be wastin' your time. All book publishers want today is crap about politicians, pimps and tarts, or wife-swappin'. Maybe later, when we've had time to think it over, but not now."

It was evident that Roland and Estelle were still shocked and disappointed, but they spoke with hints of optimism coupled with bluntness and finality. They could still manage a smile, but the old passion was gone. They seemed engulfed in an atmosphere of jovial uncertainty.

Roland looked visitors squarely in the eye, as usual, but said no more, a flicker of a smile on his face.

Estelle, in her rocking chair on the cozy back porch, put the final word to any suggestions they might return to the show again, as they had done in 1948.

"We are never going back, no matter what happens; never! Are we, Roland?" she said with a determined nod. "I'd rather pick s--t with the chickens than ever work for the Ringlings again!"

Wide World Photos

A lion cub looks on as John Ringling North (*right*) signed an agreement on November 11, 1967, to sell Ringling Bros and Barnum & Bailey Circus to the Hoffeld Corporation. Center is Judge Roy Hofheinz of Houston, Texas, and at left is Irvin Feld of Washington, D.C., two of the new owners. The signing took place among the ruins of Rome's Colosseum, often called the birthplace of the circus.

CHAPTER NINETEEN

TO SPEND AN AFTERNOON with Roland and Estelle Butler in their "retirement" was a rich and rare pleasure. While she talked frankly and intelligently on current events and made bitchy remarks against the Ringlings, Roland walked about the grounds, where a dozen sunburst wheels lay in disarray — leaning against oaks, propped against the house, or lying scattered about.

"What about all those wheels?" the friend asked. "Aren't they worth a lot as souvenirs — coffee tables, decorative pieces, or markers for the driveway as you have done, Roland?"

"I guess so, if they're in good shape. A lot of work there, but offhand I can't think of anybody who'd want the damn things, can you?"

As they walked and talked, he loosened his necktie, unbuttoned his shirt collar, and rolled up his sleeves halfway to his elbows in deference to the heat and humidity of the June afternoon.

"Now maybe I'll find time to do some of the things I should have done years ago," he grumbled. "I'll get all the stuff catalogued and maybe sell some of the crap. Tell you the truth, I don't know how much I've got, or what it's worth. I'll have to do a little advertising.

"Christ, it's everywhere! The little house is full; I've got a lot in the attic, some even in the utility room. We're cramped for space, you know. I've neglected the stuff for years; never had time."

He climbed the steps to the cottage, shoved open the balky door, and opened a window to let in some fresh air. The place reeked with the musty smell of paper and ink and stagnant air.

Here was complete disorder, with circus paper everywhere. From all indications Butler had never thrown anything away, especially if it had a circus connection.

Starting just inside the door he attacked the mounds of circusiana with grudging reluctance. Evidently his heart was not in the room but perhaps out along the Canadian border where the weather was cool and sunny now, in any one of a hundred cities and towns he knew so well, visiting newspaper friends.

He would pause briefly to glance at photographs and scan newspaper clippings before stuffing them into large manila envelopes and tossing them into odd piles. He'd thumb through posters and odd sheets of paper before shoving them into dresser drawers or cardboard boxes.

"If you can use any of this crap, for Christ's sake take it," he said. "Anything you see you want?"

"Could I help sort some of it, Roland?" the friend inquired.

He paused a moment, then put on his sheepish grin.

"Where the hell would you start?" he asked, and burst into hearty laughter.

Roland spent most of that summer listing items he hoped to sell. He then called on his friend Julian Howze in his print shop, where he placed an order for 500 copies of a catalog of circus matter.

It listed letterheads, posters, heralds, and other items at prices ranging from $1.25 to $10 or more. It wasn't complete but was a start, and he planned to add more pages. Most of the offerings were pre-1900, although he offered some window cards of later date.

The Butlers could use the cash, for none was coming in now, and they didn't want to disturb their little nest egg. Roland planned to apply for social security, but he didn't know how long the paperwork might take or how much he'd receive. Estelle did not qualify, due to her age.

Roland never broadcast his age — actually was tight-lipped about it. Once when a close friend dared ask how old he was, he hesitated a moment, looked him straight in the eye, and replied:

"I'm old enough so when I think of it the thought scares hell out of me! Does that answer your question?"

His advertisements offered seventy different classes of heralds, folders, and window cards from shows dating back to Barnum's American Museum in New York in 1864; letterheads of twenty-five circuses going back to G. F. Bailey & Co. Great Menagerie and Circus of 1866, and thirty-two circus couriers and window cards featuring the Ubangis and giraffe-neck women.

He especially liked what he called "opposition rat bills," and his collection included twenty editions dating from 1876 to 1885 — years when the L. B. Lent, Adam Forepaugh, Cooper & Bailey, W. C. Coup, Isaac Van Amburgh, and Reiche & Bros. circuses fought furiously for the entertainment dollar.

One of his favorites was from the L. B. Lent Circus in 1876 against Cooper & Bailey in Minnesota. Of it, Butler wrote;

"In its notice to the public, this bill says: 'SCOUNDRELS' who fear the light of day have, in the DARKNESS OF NIGHT and on the sabbath day, extensively circulated bills that the NEW YORK CIRCUS AND MENAGERIE, to use their own terms had 'BUSTED,' and would not exhibit in Winona, Rochester and Mankato. 'THE NEW YORK CIRCUS AND MENAGERIE WILL EXHIBIT AS ADVERTISED AT ALL PLACES AND PAY ALL JUST DEMANDS.'"

Another Lent rat sheet took local authorities to task for "granting a license to such a gang of three-card monte thieves, desperadoes and housebreakers to enter their town and be turned loose to raid the homes of defenseless citizens."

Perhaps Butler's favorite rat bill was one circulated by the Great Forepaugh Show of 1881 against P. T. Barnum's Greatest Show on Earth and Great London Circus. Butler's advertisement read:

"This outstanding item of circusiana headed 'A BUBBLE PRICKED — SOLD AGAIN!!' tells what Barnum's parade announcements promised to the citizens of Washington and Baltimore, declaring that 'Every statement made is GROSS EXAGGERATION without a single word of truth!'

"Distributed on March 28, 1881, the bill backs this up by printing 'A correct inventory of ALL THAT APPEARED IN P. T. BARNUM'S NEW YORK PARADE, MARCH 26, 1881' and asking the reader to 'NOTE THE DISCREPANCY between the PROMISED and what was REALLY GIVEN.'"

The bill, which Butler offered for $10, claimed "Forepaugh exposes fraud! Falsehood! and downright deceit! in the interest of the people."

One of the most interesting in the Butler collection was a herald circulated by S. H. Barrett & Co.'s New United Monster Railroad Shows of 1883, featuring a "Grand tidal wave of wonders, including Xerxes, largest elephant on earth.'

At this time Xerxes was competing with the elephant Jumbo, brought from London by Barnum in the spring of 1882. Butler had this comment on Xerxes:

"A large cut of the 'mastadon of mastadons' is shown in stride alongside of prancing horses, which hardly reach to the elephant's knees. The copy states that this 'moving, living mountain of flesh and blood, towering in height and strength, walks airily and jauntily with a band of twenty pieces on his gigantic back with as much ease as the ordinary horse bears an empty saddle.'"

Those "rat bills" told much about the circus business in those days, and Butler delighted in reviewing them. He offered the Xerxes herald for $4.

"That's forceful rhetoric, by God!" Roland noted. "It's pure circus, and it tells something, don't you think?"

A poster advertised by a collector as "The capture of Gargantua" puzzled Butler, who pondered whether to buy it.

"I can't recall a litho or poster termed 'The capture of Gargantua,'" he said. "It's probably one of those we got up in Sarasota when we introduced the gorilla — maybe the one of him comin' through the jungle bein' chased by pygmies. I don't need that."

He bought bundles of molding from a nearby lumberyard to frame some of his pictures. After hours of classifying items in

The Butler home in Palmetto, Florida, where they lived for 15 years. The house at rear became Roland's workshop after he left the circus in 1954. Roland insisted he was "fired."

his collection, he'd attack the framing with saw and hammer, which helped him relax and gave him a bit of exercise.

Walls of the Butler home were hung with fine works of art. Scattered throughout the house were pieces of exquisite cut glass and silver, much of it from friends all over America.

Butler was especially proud of his paintings and called visitors' attention to them. Some were gifts from Kenneth Stuart, art editor of what Butler always called "The Sat'day Post." One of his favorites was a seascape by Anton Otto Fisher.

"You like it?" he would ask, standing proud and smiling. "That's one from my friend Ken Stuart. It's a real work of art."

Roland lost none of his zest in retirement. While working with a friend on a book about the circus he wrote on November 11, 1954:

"I want to check some things as they come up, such as spelling of names. For instance, I believe Yankee Robinson's full name was Fayette Lodewick Robinson — not Lodawick — but we'll have it correct for the sake of accuracy."

Soon thereafter he reported it was neither but was spelled "Lodavick."

He also researched the White City meeting held in Chicago in the fall of 1922, which marked a milestone in American circusdom but never had the results its sponsors hoped to achieve. Under the date of August 6, 1956, Butler wrote:

"I checked that Bernard story with George Smith. In the twenties George was closer to Charles Ringling than anyone — with him all the time — and dined with him in his private car after the night show.

"Chas Ringling had advanced Smith from cookhouse coffee boy to supt. of front door in no time at all and was schooling him for the asst mgr's job. [Spellings and abbreviations are his.]

"Smith knows all about that Chicago White City meeting with Jerry Mugivan and Bert Bowers. There were several other

meetings in the Midwest that year. All of them concerned the *Billboard's* stories of circus graft that the Ringlings claimed were destroying the public's faith in the big top industry.

"Mugivan & Bowers owned the grafting circuses and had never operated any shows without graft. They were squealing like stuck pigs about old Donaldson, publisher of *Billboard*, Charles Ringling and Sam Banks, former Mugivan employee whom they claimed had turned rat for money from Donaldson or Ringling.

"Circus performers, who never shared in the spoils from graft, but were at times beaten up by 'towners' who were robbed by grafting shows, frequently worked for the Ringlings for much less salary than they would accept from Mugivan & Bowers.

"They wanted the prestige of being with the Big Show and were willing to pay for it. They also wanted the freedom from bodily harm that went with a non-grafting show and were willing to pay for that. It was hard for Mugivan & Bowers to get and hold good performers. The no-graft campaign against these shows was not helping matters.

"Mugivan & Bowers were telling performers that Ringling was going to sell out to them, and that performers would then be without jobs unless they'd play ball with M & B. Smith said that M. B. performers were spreading such crap during the graft exposure days.

"At that time the Ringlings were at their height. There wasn't enough money in the outdoor show business to buy that Ringling — B & B Circus. It stood alone at the peak of the outdoor show world and the Mugivan & Bowers shows were smaller thirty-car outfits — all on the way out. Some of their help considered them powerful but not the more intelligent ones, who sought Ringling connections.

"Most of them were with the Big Show before John even bought out those circuses. Emmett Kelly worked for Mugivan back in the '20s but didn't amount to any more than those Bernards, who never were of any consequence. Emmett became a star later.

"George Smith says the circus field is full of old 'remember when' pricks like the Bernards. He says the old farts wait until they're so old that they figure everybody who could dispute them is dead, and then they lie like sons of bitches about anything and everything that might win them attention.

"With their listeners probably unborn on the dates they sound off about, there's little chance they'll be caught up with. The deceiving old bastards ought to be making peace with God instead of deliberately leading folks away from facts.

"There's nothing to any part of their yarn nor the statement of Mugivan's about disaster & bankruptcy resulting from use of the title, etc. after Ringlings died off, in my estimation.

"Mugivan was smart when it came to those kind of explanations — he'd used them all his life to square lawless acts many times. He could convince an Eskimo to buy a refrigerator and had no trouble at all in selling any kind of a bill of goods to the sappy subjects in his fold."

Roland Butler now was in a position to reveal many circus secrets and was of a mind to do so. An inquiry about Henry Ringling, Jr., son of one of the seven brothers and also known as Henry Ringling II, brought this response:

"A big, strapping chap, every inch a Ringling in appearance, he had run the Al Ringling theater for a number of years. He also had to do with Joe McCarthy's political campaigns, with Madison, Wisc., headquarters. The last time I saw him in Madison he said he was worried about something or other regarding Joe's forthcoming election. (I wasn't much interested and don't remember details.)"

Then Roland proceeded to expound about the Gollmar Bros. Circus in these words:

"The Gollmar Bros Circus was run by four brothers in Baraboo — Walt, Fredc. (Spelled like this — one word), B. F. and Chas.

"This is the copy that was printed beneath the walrus-mustached portraits of the sons of b-----s whose show was labelled: 'Gollmar Brothers Greatest American Shows.'

"The Gollmars, cousins of the Ringlings, toured mostly in the region of the Dakotas, Iowa, Wisconsin, Minnesota and adjacent areas, as I recall. I knew Fred and Chas.

"After the Gollmars gave up in the early 1900's, the title was used by Jim Patterson, a carnival owner of Paola, Kans. The combined Patterson-Gollmar Circus, about 20 cars in size, I believe, was active in the '20s. I saw it a couple of times when with Sparks. If I'm not mistaken, Fred Gollmar was a gen. agent of this show for a while.

"The Gollmars lied like b------s in their handbills and couriers, claiming to have a circus bigger than any other in creation. I think it was never larger than 20 or 25 cars. They boasted about being cousins of the Ringlings, although I never heard mention of them from any Ringling. Guess they were on the wrong side of the tracks as far as the Ringlings were concerned.

"However, there was another Gollmar brother, not in the circus partnership, who was a physician. He was the Ringling Circus doctor for a few years, leaving the show to practice in Waterloo, Iowa."

Butler never let up in his quest for circus information, especially about the Ringlings and their relatives, and was happy to pass it on. On August 24, 1957, he wrote:

"Now I learn that Henry C. Moeller died May 22, '57, in St. Mary's Ringling Hospital, Baraboo, Wis., at age of 89.

"He, with his father, Henry, Sr., and his brother, Corwin G., operated the Moeller Carriage and Wagon Works in Baraboo many years. They built, remodelled and repaired Ringling wagons. Their last work for circuses was in 1927 when they built Sparks Circus wagons.

"The mother of Henry C. and Corwin G. Moeller was a sister of Salome Juliar Ringling, mother of the Ringling Bros and also of Magdaline Juliar Gollmar, mother of the Gollmar Bros. This makes the Gollmars first cousins of the Moellers, too.

"Henry C. Moeller trouped but one season — was a bandman with Gollmar show in 1891 — then returned to the wagon shop."

Butler then wrote about one of the most interesting shows ever to go on tour. In a letter to a friend he said:

"The name of Dick Ringling's show was R. T. Richards' Circus. It was a whale of a motorized show — run by Art Eldredge for Alf T. Ringling. Alf T. built that show and named it. Guess he named it after his son, Richard T. Ringling, (Dick), but there was definitely an 'S' on the Richards, and the apostrophe came after 'S.'

"Bernie Head, the contr. press agent I hired for the Big Show, was gen. agent of this Richards' show. Bernie worked for Alf T. with headquarters over in Alf T.'s New Jersey home. Alf T. always thought all circuses would wind up on motor trucks. That was a Ringling experiment. Way ahead of its time, but nevertheless correct enough.

"Alf T. was heartbroken about Dick, who wouldn't go near the Richards' show. I saw it in a town outside of Boston, somewhere around Marlboro, Mass. That day the show was playing the wrong town — it was advertised for another stand 15 or 20 miles away. It came to a swell lot along the highway, set up and opened up for business out in the country.

"That's absolutely true and probably the only time in circus history that such a thing happened. Alf T. spent a fortune on that venture. (All without any of the brothers' financial assistance, so I was given to understand.)"

Although he had "retired," as circus officials put it, and been "fired," as he in-

sisted, Butler never lost his concern for fellow troupers or his interest in the outdoor entertainment business. He kept informed of what went on through friends on the Ringling show and others.

One of his comforting connections was George W. Smith, with the Big Show for many years and general manager a dozen or more. Smith lived in nearby Sarasota, and Butler kept in touch with him through personal visits and telephone calls.

When Ringling Bros and Barnum & Bailey Combined Circus struck the Big Top for the last time in Pittsburgh on the night of July 16, 1956, it was a weeping, woeful event. Hundreds of men and women were out of jobs, stranded, and bewildered.

Although he never expressed his sentiments at the time, Butler was hired by Clyde Beatty-Cole Bros. Circus as publicity consultant and was happy because it put him back into the work he loved and did so well.

The Beatty-Cole show now had an advantage, but few believed that the Ringling-Barnum circus would never go out again. There was no way so much pep and bravado would go down the drain.

Pat Valdo, veteran trouper, who in some fifty years rose from clown to director of personnel, was one of the few officials available to reporters when the crippled monster reached winter quarters. John Ringling North refused to be interviewed. Valdo said:

"We will go out again. As long as there's a child, a clown, and a horse on earth, there will always be a circus."

He was right. Ringling Bros and Barnum & Bailey Combined Circus didn't go out again until spring, but it opened in Madison Square Garden on April 9, 1957, and has toured without the Big Top ever since, now performing in Red and Blue units instead of one overwhelming production.

CHAPTER TWENTY

THE RINGLING closing left the Clyde Beatty Circus the only railroad show in America. Premier animal trainer of his time, Beatty still had his cats and a private railroad car, but the circus bearing his name was owned entirely by the Monarch Circus Equipment Co., as the holding company, and National Circus Corporation, as the operating company.

Art Concello, the former triple somersault star and later Ringling general manager, held a first mortgage of about $50,000 against the operating corporation, and there was another of $16,000 owned by Frank McClosky and Walter Kernan. In addition, the corporation owed federal taxes, wages, and other obligations.

McClosky, Kernan, and others took up Concello's mortgage and were able to stock their circus with tons of talent because both the Ringling and Floyd King circuses were off the road.

Roland Butler was hired as publicity consultant and to turn out work for the show's advertisements. Other experienced and talented help included Floyd King, David Blanchfield, Eddie Howe, Count Nicholas, Robert Reynolds, Artie Walsh, Jimmy Hammiter, Howard Y. Bary, Mrs. Edna Antes, and others.

Clyde Beatty owned no part of the show but worked under contract. It became Clyde Beatty–Cole Bros. Circus and had winter quarters at DeLand, Florida. It showed under canvas for twenty-five years,

until the end of the 1981 season when it was sold and dismantled.

Butler was still working for the Beatty-Cole show when he suggested to a friend they write a book about Louis Moreau Gottschalk, whom the press agent described as "The world's most dashingly handsome idol and woman killer of his day."

Where Butler acquired such information was never divulged, but he referred to Gottschalk as "this bird," and described him in these words:

"Gottschalk was the top concert pianist in the early 1860s, and society's top ladies man on both sides of the Atlantic. He was the first of the characters that have driven the ladies mad for nearly 100 years. His life was exciting while it lasted — he lived only 40 years.

"He wrote sweetly sentimental music that youthful pianists on both sides of the oceans toiled over, and even stirred President Lincoln to a point that he had Gottschalk autograph music of 'The Dying Poet' and 'The Last Hope'....

"These pieces were written by Gottschalk before his jungle rhythms, 'Bamboula' and 'Bamamier' (Banana Tree) which made Gottschalk famous in his teens. He was the first American musical star to win the praises of the old world....

"His very appearance set the women palpitating — they came to his concerts in droves — long before Valentino and other such performers came on the scene. He used to march onto the concert stage in flawless attire, even to white gloves. He would salute the sisters with a beautiful smile beneath a lordly walrus mustache."

Evidently Butler had done considerable reading about Gottschalk. His letter continued:

"Gottschalk was born in New Orleans and had a hell of a career. Chopin declared him in a class by himself, probably referring to his music.

"If we can get some dope on him and do a story about him being a forerunner and out-doing the present day crop of band men, crooners, and others that have woven themselves into the hearts of over-sexed females, teen-agers and such as used to lap the footprints of Valentino on the sidewalk in front of Grauman's in Hollywood, it should be a beaut. . . .

"I will make a wash drawing of the bastard with bedroom eyes and all. I've felt from the beginning we could do a pip on him, linked with present day fascinators that knock the ladies cuckoo."

Rare music journals declare Gottschalk began studying violin when he was six years old and made his debut at the Salle Playel in Paris before he turned fifteen. A determined search failed to turn up any book written about Mr. Gottschalk.

Circus fans continued to write Roland Butler, and the bitter old man grasped every opportunity to express his vindictive attitude toward the Ringlings, using frank and forceful language even in letters to persons he's never met.

One of these was sent to Dr. Samuel J. Barker, eighty-one-year-old dentist in Jefferson, Iowa, on November 16, 1956. Dr. Barker had grown up with the Ringlings in Baraboo, saw their first circus performance as a boy of nine, and maintained a lively interest all his life.

Barker was preparing a booklet on Yankee Robinson, the veteran circus man who was a partner with the Ringlings during their first season and who died in Jefferson.

Butler provided details of Yankee Robinson's life from the time he was born May 2, 1818, his five marriages, and association with the Ringlings to his last days. He wrote:

"From all I have heard from old-time showmen, Yankee Robinson, whose real name was Fayette Lodavick Robinson, was a much finer type of man and better showman than any of the 5 original Ringling brothers or their 2 brothers, A. G. and Henry.

"There is no record of the Ringlings ever having contributed to the care of Yankee in Jefferson after he did so much for them. But that has been typical of the Ringlings throughout their history — just no good, heartless 'hog Dutch.'

"The father and mother were said to be a fine, God-fearing couple. Charles, the smallest, best educated and most intellectual of the brothers, had much in the way of human kindness and generosity.

"The other brothers should have been dumped down a sewer from what old-time Ringling employes, with them since their circus beginning, have often told me. They deserted many the same way they did Yankee — faithful old Ringling men told me during my many years with the organization, when John and Charles ran the show.

"While Yankee died on Sept. 4, 1884, at 3:15 p.m., the Ringling Bros official route book that year gave the date of his death as about Aug. 25. The show was in Iowa all that time and they should have had a man at his bedside while he was in Jefferson.

"It was the least the skunks could have done for the famous respected old showman who put them in the circus business."

The letter was written more than two years after the circus announced Butler's "retirement" — actually his release — and his bitterness had not diminished. His letter to Dr. Barker continued:

"Years ago John Ringling told me that old Yankee was a sick man with an advance case of Bright's disease when the Ringlings

Estelle Butler, Roland's wife for more than 40 years, who drove her husband some 750,000 miles during their years with circuses. Butler never learned to drive an automobile.

got him and they expected him to 'kick the bucket' the first year out.

"What the Ringlings wanted was the name of a well-known showman for their advertising without paying anything for it. Yankee's death was very satisfactory to them, wiping out all obligations, and they were probably happy to let the Masons foot the bill.

"I'm sorry I can't direct you to living relatives of old Yankee or tell you where he joined the Masons."

Butler's job with the Clyde Beatty–Cole Bros. Circus was not enough to keep him busy full time. He had passed his sixty-ninth birthday, and his eyesight was beginning to fail. He was getting $105 a month in social security, plus a few dollars from the sale of circus material. An order for a letterhead or Christmas card might bring up to $50.

His failing eyesight became a matter of concern to him and Estelle. Under date of

July 20, 1961, he sent this printed notice to customers and friends:

"Recently I have been hospitalized with surgical operations on both eyes. I regret that I will be unable to fill orders or handle other business until October first."

Idleness galled him, and he eagerly awaited the day he could return to his drawing board, producing Christmas cards for the coming season and other circus matter. He seldom mentioned the circus or those connected with it.

The big, old, tented Ringling Circus was no more. It played in convention halls, coliseums, and baseball parks; even performers traveled by limousine, trailer, or truck. The press department was only a memory; local publicity, and most advertising, was handled by public relations men in cities the circus visited.

Merle Evan's band had dwindled to himself and two or three other regulars, augmented by musicians hired in each city the show visited.

The circus abandoned winter quarters at Sarasota and moved to Venice, eighteen miles to the south. It was to spend little time there, coming home in late November and going out again in January.

Finally, on November 11, 1967, John Ringling North announced sale of the Ringling Bros and Barnum & Baily Circus to the Hoffeld Corporation of Delaware. It included Judge Roy Hofheinz of Houston, Texas, and two brothers, Israel and Irvin Feld of Washington, D.C.

The selling price was $8 million, and when Circuit Judge Lynn Silvertooth of Sarasota approved the terms he observed:

"Where so much of the value is centered in good will, the court is careful that interests of the beneficiaries are protected."

With typical showmanship North announced the sale at the Colosseum in Rome!

CHAPTER TWENTY-ONE

NOBODY COULD EXPLAIN WHY, but circus folk generally had an aversion to town police and considered them only one notch above sheriff's deputies on the human scale.

Conversely, the Butlers were quite friendly with Palmetto police, to the point where the chief would use the family Oldsmobile sedan on his hunting trips and would fetch them game.

From the day they moved in the Butlers were looked upon as neighbors by town police. Every day one or more would drop around to check on them, listen to her, and laugh at his stories. It was their relaxation and entertainment; a good way to kill time.

One story they often requested, and he liked to tell, concerned a man called Doctor Dee, who operated a profitable medicine show in small towns scattered throughout Alabama, Mississippi, and Arkansas. The medicine show offered outdoor entertainment but differed from circuses and carnivals as it consisted only of a little free music and jokes and a chance to buy nostrums "guaranteed to cure any ailment of man or beast."

Estelle still detested the Ringlings, called them "tightwads" or worse, and claimed, "They worked us all those years for fishcakes." The cops appreciated her attitude, on their nominal salaries, and nodded agreement. Then Butler might take over to give them a slice of rural America. It went like this:

"Doctor Jay operated from a truck with sides folded down to make a flatbed, you see? He'd park on or near the courthouse square or in front of the town hall, if there was one. He had a couple of light-skinned Negroes dressed as Indians dancin' a jig, playin' banjos or guitars, and muttering mumbo jumbo to draw a crowd.

"The doctor started his spiel by sayin' the U.S. government claims this county [naming it] has the highest rate of hookworm in the country.

"'Now,' he says, 'you know what that means? It means you may have ancylostomiasis; that's progressive anemia, and explains why so many of you are always tired, hungry, and listless.

"'Now, I'm here to warn you that hookworm is prevalent among you, and you've got to do something about it. To find out if you have this dreaded hookworm, I want you to take one or two of these capsules. They're absolutely free and they'll tell if you've got hookworm. Take a capsule tonight before goin' to bed and by tomorrow mornin' you'll know if you've got hookworm. Chances are you do.'"

Here Butler would pause to explain the capsules contained a small strip of white rubber the patient would pass first thing in the morning. The rubber was folded and would stretch to a foot or more. He or she couldn't wait to go into town and see the "doctor."

"'Now!' The good Doctor Jay would shout when a crowd gathered. 'How many of you found hookworms?' Hands would go up, amid laughter.

" 'Ah-ha; just as I thought! Now, I have here the only sure cure known to man. You passed the hookworm, but the head is still there, clinging to your insides! You've got to get rid of it, or it'll grow back like a tick on a dog. This medicine is guaranteed to get rid of the head; return you to robust health and vitality.

" 'Now, my friends, I'm not gonna charge you three dollars — the regular price you may pay in a drug store. Not even two dollars, but only one dollar. For a limited time only, my friends, you can get this guaranteed medicine for only a dollar, but I only have a few bottles.

" 'Take as directed and I guarantee within one week you'll feel healthy and well again, with all your old pep and energy. Who'll be first? Yes, sir; thank you. Next? Thank you, sir. Thank you, lady.'

"By noon," Roland added, "the doctor had sold 50 or 100 bottles and was on his way to the next town. He made a damn good livin'. His 'medicine' probably was as good as any the town druggist prescribed. Doc Jay never lost a patient, far as I know, and made a fortune."

Medicine shows were popular in the days of Model Ts and ice wagons, a real panel in the American scene. One of the most popular and profitable was run by the Bartoks, husband and wife. They operated mostly in Pennsylvania coal-mining towns and tobacco-growing communities in Virginia and the Carolinas, making sure they were there in money times.

The Bartok medicine show had an all-black cast, later went into the circus business and wintered in the community of Tallevast, northeast of Sarasota, Merle Evans said Bartok made a lot of money with his medicine show and lost it with his circus, a fact confirmed by his daughter, Bunni Bartok Perz.

Roland Butler got back to his drawing board in early October as planned. He was anxious to finish a Christmas card ordered by his friend, Floyd King, for the Clyde Beatty–Cole Bros. Circus.

King, in the circus business for more than sixty years, was press agent for Beatty–Cole, at that time the largest circus still under canvas. The tour was to end at Sarasota, and King was there to call on newspapers and radio stations and arrange for a banner to be strung across Main Street.

Butler said he'd have the card ready before the end of the month, probably in ten days. King, who, like Butler, did not drive an automobile, telephoned the Butler home on October 9 between 8 and 9 o'clock to exchange pleasantries and inquire about the Christmas card.

Butler was in the cottage at the time, and Estelle called him to the phone in the main house. In his haste, he stumbled and fell down the three steps to the ground. Estelle rushed to his side; King waited four or five minutes, he said later, then hung up.

Estelle called police, who rushed her husband to Manatee General Hospital in Bradenton, just across the river and within sight of the Butler residence. Butler was in severe pain, and police told Estelle they thought he had broken his hip.

About an hour after King's phone call and Butler's mishap, Estelle returned the call. She told King her husband was in the hospital, and the veteran circus man visited him two or three times before he left for his home in Macon, Georgia.

Being confined to a hospital bed was a new and galling experience for Roland. Visitors reported he seemed to be making normal progress but was restless and anxious to go home so he could finish that Christmas card and get on with other work.

One regular visitor was Gene Christian, former newspaperman in Miami, who for years was general agent and contracting agent for such small circuses as Beers-Barnes, Sells and Gray, and others. He handled press along with other duties as-

The Palmetto Boys Club, a $150,000 facility built with money from the Butler estate and other funds in the community of 7,500 people.

sociated with smaller circuses and had known the Butlers for years.

Once he considered going to work for Roland on the Ringling show. Roland demanded to know why, and Christian said, "Prestige."

"For Christ's sake!" Butler thundered. "It ain't worth the price. You're a hell of a lot better off where you are."

They remained friends, and now Christian visited the hospital almost daily. He was there on the afternoon of Friday, October 20.

"Hello, Gene!" Roland greeted him in his usual booming voice. "How the hell are you? You know I'm getting' out of this damn hole pretty soon now. I'm sick of it."

Butler seemed more like his old self than he had for days. They chatted for a few minutes, and a young orderly came in to help Roland get on his feet for the first time in eleven days.

"The orderly might have raised him up-

right too quickly," Gene Christian said later. "I saw it, and I believe he should have been attended by a nurse or perhaps a doctor. Three nurses were chatting down the hall about two hundred feet away, but none was in the room.

"Roland indicated sharp pain, and the orderly laid him back on the bed and went for the nurses. They came running, but it was too late. They attempted to revive him, but he was gone."

It was 3:15 P.M., October 20, 1961. The cause of death was stated as embolism, the obstruction or occlusion of a blood vessel, which may occur when an elderly patient gets out of bed for the first time following long confinement.

Christian, who lived in Bradenton, left the hospital and drove to the Butler home in less than ten minutes. Estelle's woman physician had been called by the hospital and reached the house the same time as

Christian. She put the distraught widow under sedation.

Funeral services for Butler were set for 10 o'clock on the following Monday, the same hour that services were scheduled for Laura Valdo, a circus personality for many years and the wife of Pat Valdo, director of personnel on the Ringling show.

Valdo had a boomerang act and later was a clown on the Barnum & Bailey Circus, while Laura did a wire act with her brother, Fred Mears. Valdo became assistant to Fred Bradna, equestrian director, and finally personnel director on the combined circus.

The Valdos and Butlers had been friends for nearly forty years. Laura's funeral hour was pushed up to nine o'clock in Sarasota, and Butler's moved back to eleven so mourners could attend both services a dozen miles apart.

About fifty mourners from Laura Valdo's funeral attended the Butler rites, conducted by the Reverend Mr. Fred T. Kyle, pastor of Christ's Episcopal Church.

Word of Roland Butler's passing appeared in many newspapers across the country, and tributes came from everywhere. The *Bandwagon,* official publication of the Circus Historical Society, devoted three pages to him, written by Tom Parkinson, former circus editor of the *Billboard,* author, and longtime friend.

"He was a master at drawing grinning clowns" the epitaph began, "yet he preferred taking the role of the Terrible Tempered Mr. Bang for himself. He gave us the word 'Ubangi' and made everyone aware of Gargantua.

"He was skilled in drawing the full, open style of lettering and pictorials that leaped out from newspapers pages or proved readable when viewed in twelve-sheet size from a speeding car at half a block. His art might be wreathed in scrollwork and sesquipedalianism, but it never was subdued, never unnoticed. Neither was Roland Butler. . . .

"Roland's art and his department's copy served to make the Great Wallendas a household word, made the country conscious of human cannonballs named Zacchini, and let no one overlook the presence of Tom Mix on Ringling's Sells-Floto unit. . . .

"Butler's skill in sketching clowns gave us a series of beautiful covers on Ringling's programs, but none of this mirth seemed to rub off on the artist. He was known on bill cars, in newsrooms, and back on the show for the fantastic ability and predisposition to swear. Anyone who stands out above printers, billposters, editors, and roustabouts for his skillful cursing is bound to be among the most proficient — Butler's vocabulary came full scale, in all categories — obscene, profane, and what-have-you.

"With this went a temper that was likely to flare at any time. He didn't hesitate to dress down a city editor from who he would next ask for favors in publicity. He was cynical and cutting to the point that he apparently knew how Gargantua must have felt along such lines, too. . . .

"Since his early newspaper days, Butler had been accustomed to taking on freelance work. Through the years he did many such art assignments, several of them for circuses, but in late years he claimed it was Ringling — only Ringling — that never paid him for extra duty art chores. The show counted this as part of his regular job; Butler considered it extra, and not necessarily gratis.

"This skill with the sketch pad, air brush and tiger-drawing was not to be left idle. Now many show people came to him for art work. He did a letterhead for Woodcock's elephants, another for the Circus Historical Society, then some for Beers-Barnes Circus, King and Cristiani circuses. Soon he was doing letter paper, tickets, and new posters for the Clyde Beatty Circus. Carson & Barnes has a Butler letterhead. And there are more.

"Considering his Sparks heralds, his multiplicity of circus program covers, his array of lithographs for several shows, his series of letterheads, and similar work, it may be that he has left a greater mark, a wider trail across the mass of circus printed matter than any other individual. No student of show history can ever be unaware that Roland Butler was in the field.

"Once I suggested to him that The Billboard would like to do a feature about his creations for shows in the past three or four years. Butler roared back that he'd go along with the idea but that it would have to be faked in order to mean much. I disagreed, but the story idea was dropped.

"Later, about the time Wallace Bros. Circus came out with a new Butler letterhead, I wrote again, saying now the story was a natural and Amusement Business wanted it. Butler reacted like his Gargantua. He would have no part of it and declared we were poking fun at what he felt was inferior art work done since his eyesight began to fail.

"That wasn't true, of course. The art was typical Butler and sure-enough circus. Though the story idea was dead again, it was a treat to see Butler in his hey-rube character again, full of fight and profanity."

Floyd King, one of Roland's longtime friends and greatest admirers, summed up his sentiments in these words:

"We shall greatly miss Roland. He was one fellow that will never be replaced."

When he was being hauled off to the hospital, Roland told his wife not to let anyone see the Christmas card he was designing until he could finish the job. Now that he was gone, King asked his friend Gene Christian to pick up the card and send it to Harry Anderson at the Enquirer Printing Co. in Cincinnati to be finished and printed.

The card depicted Santa Claus holding a large silver platter on which rested the Clyde Beatty–Cole Bros. Circus big top, all embellished with typical Butler ornamentations. He had flags flying from center poles, and the card was ready for final touches.

Another artist finished it and, according to King's evaluation, "Where there is blue on the side of the wall, you could tell it was not Roland's drawing."

The card quickly became a collector's item and still is a topic of discussion among circus fans. Roland Butler was a perfectionist to the end.

CHAPTER TWENTY-TWO

ESTELLE BUTLER was in shock and confusion for several days following Roland's death and remained under the care of her physician and the daily supervision of Palmetto police. Gene Christian wrote three weeks later that she seemed to have come out of her depression.

"I took my wife over to see Mrs. Butler Sunday," he said. "Both women are Irish and have something in common. The appearance of Mrs. Butler and her whole demeanor spoke of normalcy, rational well-being, and 'How the hell are you, Gene?' with a smile."

The Manatee County probate judge appointed Christian to make an inventory of Butler's circusiana. Christian reported he found one room in the cottage crammed with circus paper of every kind.

On the counterpane of a made-up double bed in another room were layers of letters two feet thick, evidently tossed there after opening, many with envelopes attached. The appraiser surmised that Roland had been piling mail on the bed for years; he said the layers were like growth rings on the trunk of a Sequoia.

The chief of Palmetto police looked over the mass of material with Christian one day and suggested to Estelle that she have it hauled to the town dump and burned! Evidently he was not a circus buff.

Christian didn't place a monetary value on what he found, but others told Estelle that if it were properly catalogued it might be sold to circus fans for a sizable amount.

She needed all the money she could get, and she now considered every scrap of paper her husband had saved to be worth good American dollars.

"I gave the whole mess away for $2,000 and got $1,000 down," she confided later.

The collection went to Paul Caldwell, a Roanoke, Virginia, schoolteacher and Roland Butler aficionado. Caldwell proposed that Butler be named to the Circus Hall of Fame, then located in Sarasota, and offered several personal items for a room honoring him — brown briefcase, hat, overcoat, letters, and photographs.

"Butler was outstanding for his bill writing," Caldwell said. "Think of the thousands of people who have stood and viewed his wonderful work. His posters were and still are an artistic triumph. . . .

"Butler was a great man and, as so often we find in men of such nature, he was a modest man. He was a humble man and often went beyond his means to help the small man out. He gave us so much for so little."

The Christmas card Butler had almost finished at the time of his passing, Caldwell said, "was a definite benediction to this man who gave 40 wonderful years to the American circus."

Within the year Butler was nominated to the Circus Hall of Fame and elected unanimously. A brief memorial service to him was held on December 29, 1962, when Estelle told the audience, "I shed many tears at the thought that my Roland has been so wonderfully honored."

More sadness and sorrow quickly followed. Their only daughter, Estelle Butler Brennan, died a few months later of cancer in New York. Then Paul Caldwell was murdered in his museum in Virginia.

Estelle Butler's health began to fail, and in July 1965 her leg was amputated. Due to her plumpness she had difficulty getting into and out of bed, even with the help of her faithful housekeeper and friend.

Capt. Harry Bates and other members of the Palmetto police force pitched in to help. They rigged up a portable pallet that could be raised and lowered by pulleys suspended from the bedroom ceiling, enabling her to get into and out of bed. With this, the plucky widow could manage.

She was a gutsy individual who never lost her fighting spirit or sense of humor. She continued to live in the white house with the green trim until she passed away on February 13, 1966.

Roland continued to receive honors from circus buffs along after he had gone to "the big lot in the sky." In addition to his being elected to the Circus Hall of Fame, a circus "tent," or club, was named for him.

The Circus Fans Association, organized in 1926 with members now scattered throughout the world, has tents in 136 cities in the United States and Canada.

The Roland C. Butler Tent No. 102 was organized in 1965, with members throughout Arizona and Nevada. It was host to the CFA international convention held in Scottsdale, Arizona, in June 1981.

The Butlers left no close survivors, and the estate went to their friends, the Palmetto police, who used the proceeds to build a fine clubhouse for the Palmetto Boys Club. It cost $150,000, and a plaque at the entrance states it was made possible through the generosity of Roland and Estelle Butler.

The Butlers, like many other circus people, had a horror of being buried in a potter's field and bought plots in Manasota Memorial Park long before they needed them.

Manasota, located in the community of Oneco southeast of Bradenton, has been in operation since this was pioneer country in 1925. It has been called Circus Cemetery because so many troupers are buried here — owners, managers, performers, and workingmen; even "strange people" from the sideshow.

There are mausoleums, crypts, graves, and urns spread over twenty-seven peaceful acres, with fifteen more reserved for expansion.

This is not a ghastly display for the hereafter but a sensible preparation for the inevitable. Circus folk resting here endured rough and rugged lives; they knew hardships, courage, loyalty, and a free spirit. To them death was and is always a sure thing, and they prepared for it the best way they knew.

A striking pink marble edifice bearing the name "Ringling" contains the remains of Charles Ringling; his wife, Edith, and their daughter, Hester. It dominates that portion of the park, and no other Ringlings are buried here.

Merle Evans, the grand old bandmaster who was still going strong when he celebrated his eighty-ninth birthday at Christmastime in 1981, has reserved crypts for himself and his wife, Nena, in the Grecian Temple, an ornate building on the park's north side. Dates are inscribed on both, and musical notes are inscribed on Evan's final resting place. Nena died June 28, 1982.

Nearby is a large plot bearing the words, "The Wallendas," and beneath that, "Aerialists Supreme." Karl and other family members are buried here, and there's room for more.

"The Family of Hannefords" is marked by a large square of marble bearing the figure of a horse. Here lies George, famous bareback rider; his daughter, Kay Hanneford Ille, with her headstone inscribed

Gene Plowden shown with some of the circus books he has written.

"Equestrienne Supreme," and other members of the troupe.

Jules C. and Stella Loyal of the Loyal-Repensky riding troupe are buried here. So are George, Henrietta, and Kunigunde Grotefent; Philip and Sabine Kreis; Texas Jim Mitchell; Laura and Pat Valdo; also Jack Leontini, who was Karl Wallenda's agent and friend for many years.

One simple marker reads: "Polydore ("Chesty") Mortier, born in Belgium." Nothing more. He is not to be confused with another clown named "Polydor," who is buried in New Jersey.

Walter G. Kernan, an official with Ringling Bros and Barnum & Bailey Circus and later part owner of the Beatty-Cole show, is buried here; so is William Yeske, longtime head of the big circus's mechanical department, and Capt. William Heyer, the riding master.

Victoria ("Vickie") Torrence, aerialist, described by Merle Evans as "the most beautiful girl I ever saw," who fell to her death in 1945, is buried here with her costume and rigging; so is her husband, who worked with her in the Cloud Ballet.

Many others who trouped with the Ringlings and smaller circuses are buried here, along with prominent men and women of other pursuits. Most circus folk are buried in the northern portion of the park, not far from the Grecian Temple, but the Butlers are in a remote area near the southeast corner.

It wasn't that they intended to shun fellow troupers, but Roland Butler probably noticed that many came to visit graves of the Wallendas, Hannefords, Loyals, and others, and he chose a spot with a typical explanation:

"We don't want people tromping over us all day long, by God! We want to rest in peace and have a little privacy."

GLOSSARY
Circus Terms Seldom Heard Off the Lot

Aba-daba — Dessert served in cookhouse.

Ace — One dollar.

Advance men — Employees who go ahead of the show to put up heralds and posters advertising the show.

Aerial ballet — Performance featuring gymnastics by chorus girls, usually on webs.

Alfalfa — Paper money.

All out and over — End of performance.

Annie Oakley — Complimentary pass or free ticket.

Auguste clown — Clumsy, slapstick clown who wears no traditional costume.

Back door — Performers' entrance to the Big Top.

Baggage horses or baggage stock — Horses used to pull heavy spectacular floats, also wagons from trains to circus lot.

Ballet broads — Circus chorus girls.

Bally — Abbreviation for ballyhooly truth; also platform used by spielers to entice crowd into tents.

Ballyhoo — Spiel in front of sideshow tent to attract customers.

Banner line — Pictorials on canvas hung in front of sideshows.

Bible, The — The *Billboard*, amusement business paper now called *Amusement Business*.

Big Bertha — Ringling Bros and Barnum & Bailey Combined Circus.

Big cage — Steel-meshed or meshed arena where wild animals perform.

Big Top — Main tent used for the performance.

Blowdown — When tents are blown down during a storm.

Blowoff — End of the performance when concessionaires come out.

Blues — General admission seats.

Boss Canvas man — Man who decides where and how tents are to be arranged on the lot.

Boss hostler — Man in charge of all horses on the show.

Bounce — Used as a verb meaning to make noise or hullabaloo.

Breaking — Elementary training of an animal.

Buckeye boy — Male native of Ohio, the Buckeye state.

Bull hand — Man who helps care for and sometimes works elephants.

Bull hook — Elephant goad with wooden handle and metal hook.

Bulls — All circus elephants whether male or female.

Bunce — Profits.

Busking — Performing in a restaurant, bar, or other public place or on the sidewalk in front.

Butcher — Refreshment peddler.

Cage boy or cage hand — Wild animal attendant who feeds and waters wild animals and cleans cages.

Calliope — Musical instrument with steam whistles played like an organ. "Calley-ope" on the circus; "Ka-lie-o-pee" by townspeople.

Carny — One working on a carnival; also corruption of carnival.

Carpet clown — One who works among the audience or on arena floor.

Catcher — Member of trapeze act who catches the flyer.

Cats — Lions, tigers, panthers, and leopards.

Cattle guard — Low seats in front of general admission seats to accommodate overflow crowd.

Center pole — First pole of the tent to be erected.

Character clown — Clown who usually dresses in tramp costume.

Charivari — Noisy entrance of clowns; also chivaree.

Cherry pie — Extra work done by circus personnel for extra pay.

Clem — A fight.

Clown alley — Men's dressing tent or aisle occupied by clowns.

Clown stop — Brief appearance of clowns while props are being changed.

Clown walk-around — Parade of clowns when they may stop and do their acts.

Come in — Time when public enters arena before performance begins.

Cookhouse — Tent where circus people have their meals.

Crumb box — Foot locker, suitcase, or box where circus workingmen keep personal belongings.

Crumb up — Used as a verb for workhand washing up, bathing, or any personal hygiene.

Dog and pony show — Small circus featuring domestic animal acts.

Dona — A woman.

Donniker, donnicker, or doniker — Circus rest rooms or outhouses.

Doors — Call meaning to let the public in.

Dressage — Art of showing trained horses; animal paces guided by subtle movements of rider's body.

Dressed — When tickets are distributed so all sections are filled and there are no empty seats.

Ducat — Ticket.

Ducat grabber — Ticket collector or door tender.

Duckie or Dukey — Box lunch.

Dukey run — Any circus run longer than overnight.

Equestrian director — Man who runs the performance from the ring floor; also called ringmaster.

Feet jump — Bareback rider who jumps from ground or teeterboard to back of running horse.

Fink or Larry — Broken novelty such as torn balloon.

First of May — Circus performer or worker in his first season.

Fighting act — Big-cat act with fast timing and a lot of noise.

Flatties — People.

Flip-flaps — Trick of flipping from a standing position to hands while bareback rider is on running horse.

Flyers — Aerialists.

Flying squadron — First section of a circus to reach the lot.

Four ways — Ways is code word for nickel, used by vendors to inform each other but not the public the price of their wares.

Framing a show — Planning a circus production.

Funambulist — Rope walker; also clown.

Funny ropes — Extra ropes to give stability and spread to tent.

Fuzz — Police.

Gaffer — Circus manager.

Galop — Fast tempo band melodies used in certain entrances and exits.

Generally useful — Phrase in circus performer's contract making him available for any work that management wants him to do.

Gilly — Anyone unfamiliar with the circus and its ways.

Gilly-galloo — Adding insult to the word gilly.

Gilly wagon — Small wagon or cart used to carry light pieces of equipment around the lot.

Gimmick — Mechanical aid hidden from the audience used to make a trick easier to perform.

Graft — A piece of work.

Grafters — Gamblers who follow a show.

Greaseball — Term of contempt for clown who does not powder his grease paint.

Grease joint — Lunch wagon in backyard where circus people and their guests buy refreshments and food.

Grotesque — Clown who wears exaggerated costume and carries outlandish props.

Guyed out — To be intoxicated; tight as a tent.

Guys — Heavy ropes or cables that support poles or high-wire rigging.

Harlequin — Clown who wears black mask and diamond-patterned costume.

Haul — Distance from trains to lot where circus tents are set up.

Heralds — Circus advertising matter which can be handed out or pasted down.

Hey Rube! — Traditional battle cry of circus people in fights with towners.

High school horse — One that has been taught special steps in riding academics.

Him-hamming — Hemming and hawing instead of speaking the truth.

Hippodrome track — Oval track inside Big Top between patrons' seats and exhibition rings and stage.

Hits — Barns, buildings, or fences where heralds and posters are pasted.

Home run — Final run of the season from closing stand to winter quarters.

Home Sweet Home — Last stand of the season.

Homy — A man. Bona homy is a good man.

Hooking — Jabbing or raking an elephant with a bull hook.

Horse — One thousand dollars.

Horse feed — Returns from poor business.

Horse opry — Any circus, used jokingly.

Howdah or Howdy — A seat, usually with a canopy, on the back of an elephant or camel.

Hulligan — Slanderous of a foreigner, especially a member of European circus troupe.

Human oddities — Sideshow of abnormal people; strange people.

Iggy — Play dumb; attitude often assumed by circus people when confronted by nosy townspeople or local police (fuzz).

Inside lecturer — Talker in the sideshow who draws attention to its wonders.

Iron jaw — Aerial acrobatic performance by person suspended by clamping jaws to a mouthpiece.

Ixnay on the ackencray, there's a flee-gee in the push — Meaning nix on the wisecracks, there's a wise guy in the crowd.

Jackpots — Tall tales about the circus.

Jill — A girl.

Joey — A clown.

Jonah's luck — Unusually bad weather or mud.

Jump — Distance between circus towns.

Jump stand — Additional booth near front door used to sell tickets during rush by customers.

Kicking sawdust — Following the circus or being part of it.

Kid show — Sideshow.

Kiester — Wardrobe trunk.

Kinker — Any seasoned circus performer.

Kish — Money, also scratch or green stuff.

Lash whip — Whip used in animal training and acts, with cord cracker at the end.

Layout man — Lot superintendent who decides location of various tents.

Lead stock — Haltered animals such as camels, zebras, and others; not horses.

Liberty acts or liberty horses — Horses trained to work in the ring without riders.

Lift — Natural bounce that lifts bareback rider to running horse.

Little people — Dwarfs or midgets.

Lot — Land rented or leased by circus for performances.

Lot lice — Townspeople who gather to watch circus unload, and linger in the backyard.

Lunge line or rope — Rein attached to horse's bridle; rope or chain attached to collar or harness of a wild beast.

Main guy — Guy rope to hold up center pole in Big Top.

Mechanic — Leather safety harness worn by flyers in practice sessions and controlled by man or woman below.

Midway — Area in front of Big Top entrance containing sideshow, concession stands, ticket and management wagons.

Mitt joint — Fortune teller's or palm reader's tent.

Mud show — Circus that travels in wagons or trucks, not on rails.

Nanty — Nothing.

Notch house — Brothel or whorehouse.

Oklahoma file — Wastebasket.

On the show — All persons connected with the circus.

Opening — Introductory remarks by an outside talker.

Oposition paper — Advertising posters put up by competing circuses.

Outside talker — Man who proclaims sideshow attractions from bally box or stand outside the tent.

Pad room — Dressing room — riders hang pads there.

Paper — Circus posters.

Parlari — Conversation among circus people.

Perch act — Balancing act performed by one or more persons while being balanced by others.

Pick out — Horse, pony, dog, or other animal trained to select objects at cue or command by trainer.

Picture gallery — A tattooed man or woman.

Pie car — Dining car on the circus train. Also privilege car.

Pinhead — Sideshow attraction with small or pointed head.

Pink slip — Notice given a circus workhand meaning he cannot work in any department and must leave the show.

Pitchmen — Salesman at concessions on the midway.

Planges — Aerialist's body swing-overs, during which wrist is placed in padded rope loop.

Ponger — An acrobat.

Popper — Cracker or snapper at end of whiplash made of flax or hemp.

Possum belly — Closed box beneath railroad car or circus wagon used for storage.

Props — Properties used by jugglers, wire walkers, and others; also elephant tubs and other items.

Pumpkin or punkin fairs — Small fairs full of pumpkins and attractive to bumpkins.

Punks — Kids or children.

Push — A crowd.

Quarter poles — Poles which help support canvas and take up slack between center and side poles.

Rat sheets — Posters or handbills which bemean the opposition.

Razorbacks — Men who load and unload rolling stock on the circus.

Read the lot — Look for tent stakes and other items after the show is over and struck.

Red wagon — Box office wagon, main office of circus; also money wagon.

Rig — To put up aerial rigging.

Rigging — Gear used to adjust apparatus used in aerial acts; also webs, trapezes; high, tight, and slack wires.

Ring banks or curbs — Wood curbing around rings.

Ring barn — Round or octagonal building with standard forty-two-foot ring at winter quarters used in training.

Ring carpet — Ground cloth used in circus ring.

Ring horse — Horse performing in center ring and trained to maintain timing despite distractions.

Ring stock — Circus animals which perform in show, including horses, ponies, camels, llamas, and zebras.

Rings — No. 1 ring is nearest main entrance; No. 2 ring is in center; and No. 3 ring is nearest back entrance.

Risley act — Foot juggling of humans.

Rola-bola — Rolling cylinder on which gymnasts perform.

Roll ups — Same as aerial planges.

Roman riding — Rider standing on backs of two horses.

Rope caller — Straw boss of a Big Top guying-out crew, giving directions to his men.

Roper — A cowboy.

Rosinback — Horse used for bareback riding; rosin keeps rider's feet from slipping.

Roustabout — Circus workingman (seldom used on show).

Rubberman — Man who sells balloons.

Run — Distance between circus towns.

Safety loop — Loop of web rope where performer places wrist in ballet numbers.

Segue — Music bridge used in changing from one tune to another without stopping.

Shandy — Electrician or member of circus electrical department.

Shill — Employee who stands in line to make ticket office look busy; also man used as decoy.

Sidewall — Canvas curtains forming walls of tent. To sidewall is to sneak into circus tent during performance.

Sky boards — Decorated boards along tops of cage wagons during parades.

Slanger — Trainer of cats.

Sledge gang — Crew of men who drive in tent stakes.

Smoke wagon — Long wagon that circles tent during teardown to collect quarter poles.

Sneaky Pete — Cheap wine.

Soft lot — Wet or muddy lot.

Spec — Short for spectacular; parade of personnel and animals inside the Big Top.

Spec girls — Show girls who appear in grand spectacle.

Spieler — Announcer.

Spindle — Metal tripod topped with revolving disk where horses or elephants may place hooves or feet.

Spindle boards — Decorated bottom edge of cage wagons used in parade.

Stand — Any town where the circus plays.

Stall act — Act used to hold an audience, often used for money or to stretch out a program.

Star backs — More expensive reserved seats.

St. Louis — Seconds or doubles on food.

Still act — A picture act.

Strip — Clown gag usually ending with unexpected removal of clothing.

Stock whip — Whip without lash but with stock and braised leather end.

Straw house — Sell-out crowd; spectators seated on straw on the ground.

Styling — Inviting applause at the end of an act by grandiose gesture frozen into a stylish pose.

Swags — Prizes.

Tableau wagons — Ornamental parade wagons.

Tail up — Command to an elephant to follow in line.

Talkers — Ticket takers for sideshow.

Tanbark — Satisfactory footing for animal performers composed of bits of tree bark.

Teardown — Taking the circus apart and packing it off to the trains.

The Big One — Ringling Bros and Barnum & Bailey Combined Circus.

The march — The street parade.

Thread the needle — Drill maneuver of horses.

Tip — Crowd of prospective customers at circus or carnival.

Toot up — Gaining attention of spectators by playing the calliope.

Tops — Tents.

Tournament — Term once used to indicate the circus spec or spectacle.

Towners — Any outsiders; townfolk.

Troupers — Circus men and women regarded with great affection, respect, and approval.

Trunk up — Command to an elephant to raise its trunk in a salute.

Turnaway — A sold-out show, overflow crowd.

Twenty-four-hour man — Advance man who works one day ahead of circus.

Under canvas — Circus playing in tents in contrast to buildings, stadia, or ball parks without a Big Top.

Virgin car — Railroad sleeper occupied by ballet girls.

Wait Brothers show — Ringlings used slogan "Wait for the Big Show."

Web — Canvas-covered rope suspended from swivels at top of tent.

Web girl — Female who performs on web in ballet sequence.

Web sitter — Ground man who holds or controls web for aerialist.

Windjammer — Any member of the circus band.

With it — Having loyalty to the show.

Write-up — Any mention of a performer or his act; never called story, review, or report.

White slip — Man fired from one job who may be hired for another type of work on same show, as opposed to pink slip.

Zanies — Clowns.

Zulu — Negro who appeared in spec.